THE FREEDOM OF LIMITATION

GOING BEYOND BY STAYING WITHIN

DR JOHN ANDREWS

RIVER PUBLISHING

River Publishing & Media Ltd
Barham Court
Teston
Maidstone
Kent
ME18 5BZ
United Kingdom

info@river-publishing.co.uk

ISBN 978-1-908393-47-0
Cover design by www.spiffingcovers.com
Printed and bound by CPI Group (UK) Ltd, Croydon, CR0 4YY

CONTENTS

DEDICATION

To my brother Alex and my “wee” daddy
who both passed into the presence of Jesus in 2013.
Our loss is heaven’s gain.
I love and miss you both.
I’ll see you soon.

ACKNOWLEDGEMENTS

Though I have written the words, so many people have helped shape them and assist me to bring them to life. Without their love, support, encouragement and service, this book would not have been possible. The people around me make me look much better than I am!

First, thanks go to Dawn, my wife, my number one fan and bestest friend in the whole wide world. I cannot imagine my life without you and I never want to experience it without you. You are the best decision I've ever made and you have helped make "my box" both enjoyable and attractive. Thank you, you're truly amazing.

To Elaina, Simeon and Beth-Anne for giving me the room to write and for your patience when I'm "in the zone". I love you.

Thank you, Sharon (www.BigPictureLiving.co.uk), for your generosity in serving yet another book and someone else's dream. I haven't forgotten about Dubai!

To Tim Pettingale for (again) expertly helping me to get a book into print and to River Publishing for taking the risk in putting their name to mine.

To TeamRenewal ... it was brief but beautiful. Thank you to those who held up my arms, walked with me through the pain and who took the time to laugh and cry with me. You know who you are; your names will always be on my heart and I will be forever grateful!

Finally, to my Heavenly Father. Because of You, I am rich beyond my wildest dreams. When I started this journey of faith some may have concluded that I was surrendering to small ambitions and a little world, but nothing could be further from the truth. Since the day I gave my all to You, You have "taken me to places I didn't know existed and given me things I could never have afforded." Having given away control to You my world has grown bigger, my heart is healthier and my experience richer. I am a better man because I had the sense to stay in Your box. Thank you.

FOREWORD

No one likes to be placed in a box or be told there's a limit to adhere to. We love to be told, "You can be anyone ... you can do anything ... you can go anywhere" and that life has "no limits".

With our modern-era cries for the "freedom" and "liberty" to do as we wish, we instinctively resist the idea of being placed under limitations or in "boxes". The culture and landscape of our day has shifted from one that establishes boundaries to one that constantly moves our boundaries to suit our whims and fancies. The Church subconsciously allows modernity to replace divine Lordship by our excessive liberation and freedom living. We accept popularity as a norm. And we allow norms to dictate the way in which Scripture is interpreted. In turn, this so called freedom dilutes the Christian's ability to truly live the life that God gives.

God has set in place guideposts and boundaries so that we can truly live an abundant life. In *The Freedom of Limitation – Going Beyond by Staying Within*, Dr John Andrews challenges our thinking on the "boxes" we are placed in. He explores how God has positioned us in the box of our unique personhood (you wouldn't want to be just anyone), the box of our God-given giftings (you can't and shouldn't do anything and everything), the box of God's purpose for our lives (avoid going just anywhere), and the box of the rhythms of work and rest (say no to 24/7 and working anytime).

In his refreshing and light-hearted style, Dr Andrews expounds the biblical design of God's box for us, starting with Jesus' example and the oxymorons of "the freedom of limitation", being #emptyfull (see chapter 7) and #happytired (chapter 10).

He helps us to uncover true freedom and a far bigger box of possibilities and fulfillment by finding and embracing our God-given boxes. The practical pointers contained in this book that help us to both discern the right boxes and enjoy this journey are "profound in their simplicity and powerful in their practicality" (to use one of the author's own phrases).

Instead of "thinking out of the box", it's time to find your God-given box.

Dominic Yeo
Senior Pastor, Trinity Christian Centre,
Singapore.

1
THE FANTASY OF LIMITLESS LIVING
[THERE'S ALWAYS A BOX]

❖

Recently I saw this comment on Twitter:

"Before 'thinking out of the box', it's always good to remember ... there is no box. #BigBoxMyth"[1]

I so desperately want to accept the idea that there are no limits to my life and that any box that does exist is simply the product of my imagination, or an inconvenience that can be easily removed. However, I genuinely believe this idea or ideal, is more the product of positive psychology than biblical theology. It sounds powerful and looks sexy, but threatens to be a "cloud without rain" for the millions of people who want to attain the reality of limitless living. The only prize at the end of this rainbow will be disappointment, disillusionment and discouragement.

From the Genesis of the Bible onwards we become aware of the existence of "boxes" or limits. Time is framed into days that have an evening and a morning; planets have orbits; the first humans have bodies; the garden of delights they are placed in has borders without and boundaries within. Even God has limits.

Yes, the all Powerful God! As a child I was taught that God can do anything, but of course He can't, He won't. His Almighty power is bordered by a moral code that He Himself cannot violate. If God goes against His own Word (in theory at least) He will implode.

When God came to us in human form, in what we describe as the incarnation – the embodiment of God in flesh, He created limitations for Himself that could not be circumvented. Jesus could only be in one place at one time. He needed to eat, rest and sleep. He didn't float around, He had to walk. He had to learn the languages of His day, pay His taxes to Caesar and be a dutiful son to His parents. He was limited by time, having to wait until He was 30 years old before He could begin His ministry. His ministry remained largely within the geographical boundaries of Israel. Then, when His body was beaten and pierced, it died!

Limits and boxes have always been part of the human experience from the very beginning, and therefore should not be an issue of unnecessary concern to us. The key is recognising we have limits, but by engaging with God's timeless truth and His relentless purpose for our lives, we can live so well within those limits that it seems like we're living beyond them. In other words, we can go beyond what we think is possible, if we stay within the God-designed boxes of our lives. He can do more with us and through us in a box, that we can do on our own, outside of the box!

The fantasy of limitless living is alive and well in the Church and we must have the courage to address this myth and come to a dynamic, life-giving understanding that we all live in boxes; that there are authentic, necessary limitations to all our lives, but that we serve a God who can not only work within those limitations, but allow us to see that the boxes are bigger than we thought and be able to do more than we can imagine.

In order to move from the empty fantasy of limitless living, into the reality that we all live in a box, we must face and conquer four key myths.

Myth #1: I can be anyone

I remember going to London to watch a show with my oldest daughter. As we walked around the packed, energised streets of our Capital, my daughter made an interesting comment. "You can be anything you want to be in London," she observed. Of course, that statement was both right and wrong at the same time. It was right to conclude that in the Big City a person can throw off their shackles and be anything they want to be. For some people this will be a truly liberating experience, perhaps allowing the world to see who they are for the very first time. However, the reality remains that no matter who we want to be or would like to be, we cannot escape the person we truly are!

When God made the first humans, He made them both in His image:

"So God created man in His own image, in the image of God He created Him; male and female He created them." (Genesis 1:27)

Yet when the serpent came to them, at the heart of his temptation was an issue of identity:

"For God knows that when you eat of it your eyes will be opened and you will be like God, knowing good from evil." (Genesis 3:5)

One of the tragedies of this story is that the woman was asked to reach out to be someone she already was (she could not be more like God), and in doing so, stepped beyond the God-designed identity-boundary for her life. As she stepped out of her box, she became someone God never intended her to be.

The truth is, you live in a box of personality. You are a unique and special individual. There is no one in the whole of human history that has been like you and when you die, your like will never be seen again. Yet so many of us try to escape who we are in order to be someone else. We expend immense levels of energy to cover, hide, dress up and change ourselves. Yet the reality is, we cannot escape who we truly are.

God is not afraid of who you are. In fact, He delights in your unique personhood. He declares that you are "fearfully and wonderfully made" and that there is no one like you in the whole universe. He wants you to reject the myth that you can not simply be yourself, or that you can walk away from your God-designed identity and be whoever you want. Rather, He wants you to embrace the glory of your design. He wants you to work with Him to see that by staying within the box of who you are, you can go further than you ever dreamed possible.[2] Within the box of our personhood, we can become bigger and better than we ever dreamed.

Myth #2: I can do anything

As I write this book I am 47 years old and I have arrived at the conclusion that if I haven't got it, I don't need it. I've come to the realisation (and peace) that there are some things I can't do. No matter how hard I try, I know that certain things will never be a reality, because the God-given gifts and skills I have just won't allow me to excel in areas for which those gifts were not designed. I would have loved, for instance, to have scored the winning goal for Liverpool in the Champions League final (against Manchester United of course). I have both dreamt about it and rehearsed it in the park. But I know it will never happen, because I'm not very good at football! Similarly, no matter how hard I pray to have a baby (not that I am ... 3 is plenty), I know it won't happen, because as a man I don't have a womb. It would be amazing to jump out of an airplane without a parachute, but I know I won't, because I just can't fly. I know these are silly and rather extreme examples, but I've met so many people trying to doing things with gifts they do not have, and usually doing it badly. Eugene Cho said, "The person that tries to do everything will do nothing well. Focus on a few things and do it (sic) well. Know it. Breathe it. Love it. Live it."[3]

No one can do everything. No one should do everything. No one is designed to do everything! So why are you trying? In his book, *The 80/20 Principle*, Richard Koch explores how individuals and organisations can "achieve more with less". But in order for this to happen, tough questions have to be asked and decisions made that allow us to realign our lives to what is truly important – rather than being driven by the urgent or waylaid by the frivolous. To get to the heart of the key opportunities in our lives we should constantly ask,

- "What is the 20 per cent that is leading to the 80 per cent?
- What are the vital few inputs or causes, as opposed to the trivial many?
- Where is the haunting melody being drowned by the background noise?"[4]

Covey described this in terms of moving our lives from the urgent to the important, ensuring that most of what we do is both what we're meant to be doing and actually good at doing.[5] As Henry David Thoreau put it, "It is not enough to be busy, we must ask: 'what are we busy about?'"

Today we live under the myth of multitasking. My youngest daughter tries to convince me that she can do her homework while listening to iTunes, while watching iPlayer, while on Face Time with her friends. For her this is the new normal, where one can text and talk at the same time and where one can post to Instagram while eating dinner! It all sounds plausible and looks doable, but don't be fooled. We're not really multitasking, we're task switching – and they are two completely different things. As Christian Jarrett put it, "...multitasking is a productivity drag masquerading as an efficiency booster."[6]

If we're not careful, multitasking becomes a disguise for a muddled task and an unclear purpose. We're trying to do everything and we end up doing nothing well. We can get away with this for one day in the office, but we don't want this to become a pattern for life, convincing ourselves that we can do anything, when really most of us can only do one or two things really, really well. Too many are trying to escape the box of their gifts, aspiring to use gifts they don't have, for tasks they're not designed for ... and even when they work really hard to get it done, it will never be their best, nor the best!

Myth #3: I can produce any time

I love my iPhone. In truth, I use it less as a phone and more as a mini-computer. If I analysed my usage, it would be 90/10 in favour of non-phone use! Ten years ago we all had phones that were just phones, but now we're carrying around pocket-sized technology that is truly breath taking in its capacity. Many of us live in a world of wall-to-wall Wi-Fi (in fact, we often won't go into a coffee shop that hasn't got Wi-Fi). We're more connected than we've ever been and, as a result, we are more contactable and vulnerable to interruption. All of this is only one small part of what is becoming for many of us a 24/7 treadmill, resulting in longer days (whether we're in the office or not), emails in bed, Facebook at breakfast, Twitter at the gym and calls in the park. As James Victore put it, "The gym and the park are no longer places for personal development or reflection, but just another place to 'check-in'."[7]

For Jews and Christians, the idea of "Sabbath" centres around one day in a week set apart for rest and "re-creation". Today, as we are being forced to develop a theology of technology, we need to be intentional about "technology Sabbaths" – times and places when we turn off the phone, shut down the Internet and give our lives time to rest, reflect, re-create and re-focus! Writing within a secular business context, I love how Tony Schwartz puts it: "...human beings aren't meant to operate continuously, at high speeds, for long periods of time. Rather, we're designed to move rhythmically between spending and renewing our energy."[8]

You can't produce all the time or any time for that matter. You're not a machine (and even if you were, you would still need a break), you're a human being and your physicality is part of the box you are in. If we ignore the needs and fragility of that physicality, then we abuse its potential to help us achieve all that God has designed us for. Non-stop working will eventually lead us into dead-stop living. We must give our minds the time to defrag and recoup. We must allow our bodies the opportunity to recover and re-create, and we must allow our souls to catch up with our relentless pursuit of business, activity and noise. As Victore concludes, "...the heroes of the next generation will be those who can calm the buzzing and jigging of outside distraction long enough to listen to the sound of their own hearts..."[9]

24/7 is not biblical, natural, normal, possible or sustainable. God has placed a box around your day and a rhythm boundary around your week, so that you understand you're not invincible, but vulnerable. By creating a designated "day of rest" God constructed a box in which He asked humanity to live. But, of course, we know better and history has demonstrated our profound ability to mess with something that is profound in its simplicity and powerful in its practicality, to come up with an alternative that is utterly bankrupt. Stay in the box of, "I can't produce any time" and you'll probably be happier, produce more and live longer than you dreamed.[10]

Myth #4: I can go anywhere

Professor Howard Hendricks mentored hundreds of pastors and leaders and his "confession" is truly striking. He writes,

"As a young leader, my biggest mistake was allowing my time to be eaten up with things outside my core competencies. I wanted to set the pace for others, to demonstrate that nothing was beneath me, so I devoted an inordinate amount of time to things I wasn't good at – things I'd never be good at. At the same time, I invested little energy into developing my strengths...

Finally, I realised that my true value lay within the context of my giftedness, not the number of hours I worked. There were some balls I'd no business juggling.

When I finally got the courage to let them fall to the floor, I began to excel in juggling the two or three balls I was created to keep in the air in the first place. And the amazing thing is, people came along and picked up the other balls. What I couldn't relinquish were the opportunities they'd been waiting for."[11]

Many of us will identify with his admission. I'm sure we've all allowed our lives to be "eaten up with things outside our core competencies". Who among us has not done things more to impress others than fulfil our purpose? How often have we tried to keep too many balls in the air simply because we believed that we alone could juggle them and that those around us would never be able to do it like we could?

The "anywhere" I speak of here is not geographic. It's much more important than that. This is the anywhere of purpose. Moving in the direction God designed for us and doing the things we were truly meant to achieve. David put it this way:

"All the days ordained for me were written in your book before one of them came to be." (Psalm 139:16)

In other words, David understood that he wasn't just "fearfully and wonderfully made" (same passage verse 14), but he was made for a purpose and that how he was made was inextricably linked to why he was made! David's identity was linked to his destiny – who he was, connected to why he was here!

David, like us all, could have written his own book. God in His infinite wisdom has granted each of us freedom of will and sometimes we choose for Him while most times we choose for ourselves. We all want to write our own book, but God wants us to understand that He has written a book for us. Not set in stone, reducing our lives to a fatalistic play, but rather His preferred purpose, which He wants us to freely embrace. However, His book (or box) has limitations, boundaries, things we can and cannot do. If we choose His purpose, then it automatically restricts us from our own. If we go His way, then we must abandon all other ways! This feels like a restriction, but the Bible describes it as freedom. Jesus put it this way:

"For whoever wants to save his life will lose it, but whoever loses his life for Me and for the gospel will save it." (Mark 8:35)

This is a box. If we choose to climb into this box, then we're automatically saying no to a lot of other "opportunities". Yet Jesus is teaching us that rather than restricting us and making us smaller, His box, the box of His purpose, will give us life, enlargement, incredible opportunity, meaning and fulfilment. Like Doctor Who's Tardis, it may look small on the outside, but it's huge on the inside. But we never discover that reality until we venture inside!

It was Warren Buffett who reportedly said, "The difference between successful people and very successful people, is that very successful people say no to almost everything." Of course, the reason they can say no, is because they've already said yes to something else – something bigger and better, something that empowers them to say no to "lesser" offers, thus ensuring their lives are not distracted by lesser things.

Let's get rid of the #BigBoxMyth and come to a biblical understanding of how life actually works. We all have boxes, but the key is discerning,

- Which boxes are man-made and which are made by God?
- Which boxes can be smashed and which boxes must we have the courage to learn to live within?

Not every "box" is bad. Learning to stay within our God-designed box may not only save our lives, but empower us to live the life we always dreamed of, and which God has always wanted for us.

Summary and Reflections

I can be anyone

"The truth is you live in a box of personality – you are a unique and special individual. There is no one in the whole of human history that has been like you and when you die, your like will never be seen again."

God does not tolerate who you are rather He celebrates who you are. A clearer understanding of your identity will help you engage with your destiny.

What aspects of your personality do you consider as a strength – and why?

What aspects of your personality do you consider a limitation – and why?

I can do anything

"No one can do everything – no one should do everything – no one is designed to do everything! So why are you trying? "

When it comes to the limits of your abilities, what boxes are 'God-made' and what ones are person-made?

I can produce any time

"Non-stop working will eventually lead us into dead-stop living."

Does the rhythm of your life enhance or reduce your productivity?

I can go anywhere

"If we choose His purpose, then it automatically restricts us from our own. If we go His way, then we must abandon all other ways!"

If you had the power to focus on one key area of purpose in your life, what would it be and why? What needs to change for that focus to crystalise?

Footnotes:

1. Twitter, 1/04/14
2. For more on this theme check out my book Identity Theft – Finding the Missing Person in You, New Wine Press, 2008.
3. Eugene Cho, 11/04/14 Twitter
4. Richard Koch, The 80/20 Principle: The Secret of Achieving More with Less, Nicholas Brealey Publishing, Kindle book, p.649, 2007 (first published in 1997)
5. In his book, Seven Habits of Highly Effective People.
6. Manage Your Day-to-Day: Build Your Routine, Find Your Focus & Sharpen Your Creative Mind, edited by Jocelyn K. Glei, Amazon Publishing, 2013, p.85
7. Manage Your Day-to-Day, p.162
8. Manage Your Day-to-Day, p.50.
9. Manage Your Day-to-Day, p.162
10. For more on the power of rest, check out my book First Day, Discovering the freedom of Sabbathcentric Living, River Press, (and on Kindle), 2011
11. Word for Today, UCB, 02/03/14

2
FOLLOW THE LEADER
[EVEN JESUS HAD A BOX!]

Surely Jesus didn't live in a box?

After all, if there's one person who could have lived a limitless life within a human context it's Him, right? A casual glance at the Gospels gives the impression of a man on a mission for whom there are no boundaries or limitations.

But a closer, more considered reading of the text shows that the God-man also has to contend with His own boxes. However, He addresses them so well that at first we don't even notice they're there. But they are! Too often we view Jesus only through the lens of His deity and therefore miss the power of His humanity. Though a limitless God, He learned to live and operate successfully within the limitation of His humanity, demonstrating that amazing things are possible even when confronted by the reality of boxes and boundaries. We may not like to think about it or admit it, but even Jesus had a box! In fact, from the Gospels, I want to show you that Jesus, God-incarnate, had to contend with at least five major boxes.

1. The Physical Box

"The Word became flesh and made His dwelling among us." (John 1:14)

I love how the Message Bible puts this: "The Word became flesh and blood, and moved into the neighbourhood." The mesmerising miracle of the incarnation is that God the Son became one of us. The immeasurable glory of the eternal, all-powerful, all-knowing, all-present, self-existent Creator God, was poured into a baby in a teenager's womb and was born and lived among us! Millions of words have been written around this history-changing event and though I cannot fully grasp with my finite mind the mystery of the incarnation, I celebrate its magnificence! At the heart of the incarnation, however, is a paradox: God the Son, who in His pre-incarnate state lived (within His own character and code) a limitless existence, is now "boxed in" by a human body. For the first few years this body would make Him almost entirely dependent on other human beings for His very survival, and even when He learned to stand on His own two feet, His body-box meant that God-in-flesh could only be in one place at one time, and would get tired, hungry, weak and lonely. When the sun shone His skin would burn and when the winter came, He would shiver just like everyone else. When cut He would bleed, when beaten He would bruise and, nailed to a cross, He would die!

We might not think of His body as a box, but it was. Jesus had to learn to live within and make the most of His human limitation. He has to rest, sleep, take care of what He consumed, plan His journeys carefully and give Himself every chance to succeed within His human condition. His God "part" didn't override His humanity. Rather, it lived within it. Divine Duracell batteries didn't operate Jesus! He didn't take the Divine flight option instead of walking (all of which was totally possible). He was so like us in every way that when the word started to get out that He was, in fact, something "other" than one of us, most people who knew Him just couldn't believe it!

For approximately 33 years, Jesus lived successfully with His body-box.

2. The Place Box

"Then He went down to Nazareth with them and was obedient to them." (Luke 2:51)

If you and I were to go back to 1st Century Israel, find a coffee shop with Wi-Fi access and Google "Nazareth", we'd probably be left scratching our heads. In the relatively small world that Jesus lived in, Nazareth wasn't even on the map – a measure of its insignificance. Jesus spent most of His life in a village of less than 300 people, far from the trading routes of its day, tucked away deep in a valley. An unfashionable postcode in an undistinguished region. Jesus lived in a nowhere sort of place! The big schools, the great opportunities and the important people were down south in the City, but Jesus spent the vast majority of His extraordinary life, tucked away in a village that time had forgot.

Dr Luke makes it abundantly clear (the only Gospel writer to do so), that Jesus didn't waste His time while in this place-box. We are not only told that He lived "under the orders" of His parents (the idea behind the word translated "obedient"), but that He engaged with His world and made the most of the apparent lack of opportunity. We are told that Jesus, "...grew in wisdom and stature, and in favour with God and man" (Luke 2:52). Jesus grew intentionally, deliberately, on purpose and with purpose in mind. He didn't sit in the corner and sulk, having been taken from His moment in the spotlight at Jerusalem, when the eyes of scribes and scholars were on Him. Rather, He obeyed, He served, He engaged, He contributed and, most of all, He grew. In those 18 years of silence leading up to His baptism at the age of 30, Jesus excelled in the ordinary, embraced responsibility and grew deliberately! Jesus made the most of the place-box He found Himself in.[1]

Too many lament their place-box (and I'm not minimising the challenges your place represents), but while we're lamenting we're missing the opportunity for living. The more we long to get away, the less we live well where we are. If we keep saying that God can't work where we are, in our postcode-from-hell place-box, then the chances are He won't! Jesus' luck tapped out when He drew the Nazareth short straw, but He refused to allow the box He grew up in to distract Him from His purpose or restrict Him in His growth.

For approximately 30 years, Jesus lived successfully in a place-box.

3. The Process Box

"Now Jesus Himself was about thirty years old when He began His ministry." (Luke 3:23)

Imagine the scene. You've had three of the most exhilarating days of your life, rubbing shoulders with experts in their field and engaging your talents, gifts and knowledge at the epicentre of your world. Everyone who hears you is amazed at your ability and phrases like "prodigy ... exceptional ... for His age He's the best we've ever heard" are floating around the debating area.

You're just getting into the groove when you hear your mother's voice:

"Son, why have you treated us like this? Your father and I have been anxiously searching for you." The implication being, "Hey Son, enough already. It's time to come home!" (Luke 2:48).

At 12, Jesus had the attention of some key members of His religious world – a world that He would eventually clash with and challenge. There is no doubt in my mind that keen teachers and significant influencers would have spotted the talent in the young Galilean and salivated at the prospect of such a mind in their school. But before contracts could be drafted the "boy" was gone, back up North to God knows where! Though it's clear from the Temple experience that Jesus knew His purpose – "Didn't you know I had to be in my Father's house?" (Luke 2:49) – He also knew it wasn't His time. In fact, it would be another eighteen years before His time would come. Even with all that talent and all that God inside Him, even Jesus couldn't just operate to His own schedule. He had to learn to submit to the process-box and wait for God's time.

I love how Jesus puts it in the context of the full flow of His ministry:

"My time is not yet here; for you any time will do." (John 7:6)

For many of us this idea of time is at the heart of so much frustration and tension. We think that "because we can, we should", but as Jesus shows us, there are times when we clearly can, but the time is not right because God's process is not yet complete.

I've had the joy of travelling all over the world and one of my favourite regions in the world is the Far East. I've visited Singapore, Malaysia, Myanmar and the Philippines many times.

They are all so exotic and different, and the food ... yes baby! However, the big down side with the Far East is that it's so far away from the UK! As much as I love flying, one cannot ignore the fact that in order to get to where I want to go, I have to make a significant journey to get there. If only I could just click my fingers and arrive! There have been many moments on a long-haul flight when internally I have echoed the words I used to say as a boy to my mum and dad from the back of the car: "Are we there yet?" We all want to be there, wherever we think there might be, but we have to understand that we don't just arrive there, we journey there – and sometimes that journey of process will feel like a box, a restriction and a limitation.

One of the hardest lessons in life we have to learn is that the process is as much a part of our purpose as the purpose itself. Too often we focus on where we want to go while fighting the pathway that's going to take us there. When we know we're going to be on a plane for the next fourteen hours, we need to lock it down and accept it as part of the "pleasure" of getting us to our exciting, exotic destination. If we don't, fourteen hours will feel like fourteen years and "process" will feel more like "torture" than the vehicle to our success.

Many fight the process-box. Jesus could have said, "I'm ready, so why can't I preach and teach now?" and in truth, few would have argued with the cool kid from Nazareth. But had Jesus launched His ministry at 12, the greater purpose of God would have been lost and the world would look very different from how it does today.

Don't rush ... rest! Embrace the process-box and live present within it. Stop longing for tomorrow and start maximising today. The walls of the process-box will start closing in on you if you continue to fight it, but when you embrace it and live well within it, though the box is still there, it won't feel so small.

Through the years of obscurity, Jesus lived successfully within the process-box.

4. The Purpose Box

"My food is to do the will of Him who sent Me and to finish His work." (John 4:34)

With the talents and abilities that Jesus possessed, in theory at least, He could have been anyone and done anything. I'm sure that's what some positive thinking guru would have told Him (for a fee, of course!). However, Jesus came to an understanding that all He was, all He had, and all He could do was for a unique purpose – the purpose specified by His Father. From the above verse, Jesus could have eaten any food, but He chooses to order off the menu prescribed by the Father.

There was certainly other food on the menu! The devil offered Him the kingdoms of the world if He would just bow and worship him (Luke 4:5-6), and the people wanted to make Him their king because, ironically, He provided them with lunch (John 6:14-15). However, Jesus refused all of this because He had decided to live within the purpose-box in which He had been placed. The Father's food had now become His food and Father's work had become His will.

It is easy to miss the power of this truth, but we should pause to consider it carefully. The irony is that in some cases even the purpose of God, which we know to be right and true, can feel like a box to us. Our marriage, our job, our ministry, our position, our opportunities can, if we are not careful, feel like a box – especially when we listen to those who proffer something beyond those boundaries. Satan offered Jesus an emperorship and the people desperately wanted a king. Compared to being an itinerant Rabbi, dependent on gifts of charity or part-time work carried out by His friends and disciples, surely one would have been a fool to turn it down?

Have you ever had the experience of sitting in a brand new car, either in the show room or owned by a friend? The smell, the gadgets, the feel, the ride, the cool badge ... it's all wonderful and designed to wow you. Then you climb back into your old (it was old when you bought it), high-mileage, worn out car. On the drive home you notice every rattle, the scuffmarks the kids have left, and the smell ... that'll be the dog! Suddenly, the car you loved up to that moment is sensing it might be heading for the scrap yard in the sky. Why? The impact and the allure of "something more", something apparently better, something that deep down you've always wanted. I have discovered in my life that offers of distraction have rarely come from some weird and unexpected area or have tried to take me in the opposite direction. The most subtle and dangerous moments of my life have been when what is being offered feels right, looks right and isn't a million miles off where I think I'm going anyway. The devil knows that if I'm called to leadership in the Church, I'm not likely to sign a contract for a world famous rock band or football club (although I'd be seriously tempted to sign for my beloved Liverpool #YNWA!). The most dangerous sort of distractions are those that offer something in the ballpark of where we already are and what we already believe.

Isn't that what happened to Jesus? What the devil offered Him, the Father would ultimately give Him anyway. The kingdoms of the world would one day be His. What the people offered Him, the Father would ultimately give Him anyway. He would reign as King of kings and Lord of lords! Jesus got the kingdoms of the world and became King of kings because He stayed within the purpose-box of His Father. He refused the other delicacies on offer and He stuck with the menu the Father placed before Him.

In the midst of His ministry, Jesus lived successfully in the purpose-box!

5. The People Box

"'Where did this man get these things? What's this wisdom that has been given to Him? What are these remarkable miracles He is performing? Isn't this the carpenter? Isn't this Mary's son and the brother of James, Joseph, Judas and Simon? Aren't His sisters here with us?' And they took offence at Him." (Mark 6:2-3)

Take a very close look at the above verses. These two verses essentially contain six questions and are split into two clear categories:

The first three are a recognition of what Jesus has done:

"Where did this man get these things? What's this wisdom that has been given to Him? What are these remarkable miracles He is performing?"

Within the questions is the undeniable truth that the young man standing before them, whom they know as Jesus, has somehow attained a dynamic spiritual authority. He has become very smart all of a sudden, and is doing undeniable miracles! This is the point when surely everyone should jump up and down with joy and embrace the man of God. But no, they get stuck because of the following three questions:

"Isn't this the carpenter? Isn't this Mary's son and the brother of ... Aren't His sisters here with us?"

Even though they clearly acknowledged His authority, wisdom and power, they refused to accept these things because of His human, mundane, ordinary context. "He seems to be doing amazing stuff, but it can't be true because He's a carpenter and His family are known to us!"

Tragically, instead of accepting Him, they took offence at Him. Why? They couldn't get beyond what they knew about Him in order to embrace what they saw in Him.

The ministry of Jesus was being threatened by a people-box, created by the opinions, ideas and beliefs of others. It is interesting that in His own town of Nazareth, He struggled to do any miracles, but eighteen miles or so down the road at Capernaum (which became His northern ministry base), He did numerous miracles. Moving over to Capernaum He not only crossed a border, but escaped from the boxes that others tried to create for Him and wanted Him to live within.

All His life, but especially during His three-year ministry, Jesus had to contend with the boxes others wanted to make, boxes created by perceptions, beliefs, fears, hopes and aspirations; boxes that ranged from the sublime to the ridiculous and boxes that constantly threatened to derail and destroy the purpose for which Jesus had been called.

This is why it is so important to understand the Father's purpose for our lives, so that we can address the boxes that others will always seek to make for us. People will always have an opinion about who we are, what we can and cannot do, where we can and cannot go. Even when we're doing what we believe we should be doing, there will still be the opinions regarding what and how we are living. This will never go away until the day we pass-away! Though it is important to listen to the counsel of godly, wise people who know how life works, we must be careful when listening to those whose only ambition is to box us in and restrict us from becoming the best we can be.

Jesus refused to be put in other people's boxes. The only box He was prepared to live in was God-shaped. His actions may have displeased some of the people around Him, but they brought pleasure to the One Person that truly mattered: His Father!

So what do we learn from Jesus and His boxes?

Lesson #1: The box doesn't need to be a barrier

It feels almost sacrilegious to suggest that Jesus lived in a box, and yet as we've seen quite clearly, He did. But we've also observed that He didn't allow the boxes He lived within (or which were put on Him) to form a barrier to the things He knew He could do or the person He knew He was. The reason we don't think of Jesus living behind barriers is because they don't seem that apparent to us; because Jesus in fact reconciled the tension created by them, but still learned to live successfully in spite of them. Jesus teaches us that either we can allow our physical-box, place-box, process-box, purpose-box and people-box to become barriers to our lives, or we can find ways in which to address them, live with them and make the best of them. Jesus teaches us that the boxes in our lives cannot be ignored, but neither do they have to become excuses. Limitation need not become loss and restriction does not need to result in resignation!

Lesson #2: You can live well whatever the box

Jesus lived His life well. In fact, He lived His life so well that we don't tend to notice the boxes. We forget that He could only be in one place at one time and that He didn't start what we call His ministry until He was 30 years old; that He had numerous offers and opportunities to be successful but refused them. We just tend to think that because Jesus was God, He sailed effortlessly and relentlessly towards His goal and that His success was totally inevitable!

The reality, of course, was that nothing was a foregone conclusion. The Father's purpose and plan was reliant on Jesus getting and sticking to the plan. Jesus, God the Son in flesh, had to learn to live within His boxes and learn to live well. He couldn't go AWOL or suddenly check out of His humanity and draw on the God-stuff within Him. Jesus had to stay within His prescribed boxes to allow the purpose of God to work.

Jesus teaches us that we can live well in the ordinary; that we can be productive in the routine; that we can excel in the mundane and be bigger than our postcode. Jesus offers hope and an example to each of us as we try to make the best of the box we're in and grow in the environment that surrounds us. Jesus teaches us that living well is less about what is around us and more about what is within us.

I once saw a fridge magnet that said, "How can I fly like an eagle when I'm surrounded by turkeys?!"

Sounds funny and sort of right, but it's a load of old nonsense. One day we'll stop taking life lessons from fridge magnets and start taking them from the Bible. The Bible and Jesus teaches us that even if we are surrounded by turkeys, if our DNA is that of an eagle, we can fly. Our flight is not determined by our environment, but by our INvironment. Jesus, in His world of boxes, encourages us to believe that what is within us matters more than what is around us. He lived well in a village that didn't have a postcode. We can live well wherever and whatever the box!

Lesson #3: The box may limit you, but it doesn't limit God

Jesus grew up in a nowhere place, never travelled more than 150 miles from that village in any one direction, and He rarely strayed beyond the borders of His country, situated on the eastern edge of the Roman Empire. He lived in a world before phones, television and, dare I say it, the Internet (such a world did once exist). Yet, He is arguably the most famous, most worshipped, most followed and most celebrated person in the history of the world. Love Him or hate Him, it's hard to escape Him in human history.

Yet His impact is disproportionate to the boxes He lived in. If we were to assess His boxes, we could never in our wildest dreams have predicted the influence that He would bring to bear on His world. Jesus teaches us that although the boxes we're in might limit us, our boxes don't limit God. If one was seeking world domination, then Jesus was born at the wrong time, in the wrong place, to the wrong people, with the wrong message! However, when we add in the God-factor, everything changes. It seems that God can save the world through a physical person who only lived for 33 years. It seems God knows where Nazareth is, even if Google doesn't. It seems that God's timing is perfect, even if we think His clock has stopped. It seems that God can do a great job in and through us, even if everyone else thinks it's a crazy idea. It seems that where the box stops ... God starts! It seems that if we can live well within the box, God can do miracles beyond our wildest dreams beyond the box. It seems that when the box comes to an end, God just keeps on going.

One of our weaknesses as humans is that we generally have an inflated view of our own self-importance and influence. We tend to think that everything relies on us and if we don't do it, it will never get done. The truth is, God was running the universe before we were born and He'll still be doing a great job when our bones are dust. It is not our job to do everything – it is our job to do the thing He wants us to do and leave the rest to Him. Jesus stuck to the plan and ultimately saved the world by staying within His Father's prescribed boxes. If we will have the courage to stay within God's boxes for our lives, our impact and influence will go further than we ever dreamed possible. ,Because when and where our box stops, that's when and where our God starts!

Summary and Reflections

Even Jesus had a box!

"Though a limitless God, He learned to live and operate successfully within the limitation of His humanity, demonstrating that amazing things are possible even when confronted by the reality of boxes and boundaries."

Why is it difficult for us to accept Jesus lived within any box?

Lesson #1: The box doesn't need to be a barrier

"Limitation need not become loss and restriction does not need to result in resignation!"

What are the positive limitations in your life? What limitations are actually helping you to focus your abilities and opportunities?

Lesson #2: You can live well whatever the box

"Our flight is not determined by the environment, but by our INvironment."

If you couldn't escape the box (or boxes) you are currently in, what could you change in your thinking and behaviour to make sure you make the best of the box you are in?

Thought Change: ________________________________

Action Change: ________________________________

Thought Change: ________________________________

Action Change: ________________________________

Lesson #3: The box may limit you, but it doesn't limit God

"One of our weaknesses as humans is that we generally have an inflated view of our own self-importance and influence."

Where your ability stops, God's power begins. Invite God into the limitation you feel. Recognise that as you do what you can, He will do what He can. Give praise for what He is doing and can do in and through your box.

Footnotes:

1. In my book 2:52 – Learning to Grow on Purpose, published by River Publishing in 2012, I explore fully the four key areas in which Jesus grew from Luke 2:52 and how we can learn and apply those lessons to our own lives.

3
SWAPPING BOXES

[LET GO AND TAKE HOLD]

The first time we meet the Apostle Paul in the New Testament he's called Saul and he seems to be a passive bystander to a gruesome crime. A young man called Stephen (probably a friend of Saul's) is being executed, soon to become the first official, post-resurrection martyr for the cause of Christ. Stephen's incredible sermon apologetic provoked a reaction so aggressive and fierce that it resulted in his death and Dr Luke tells us,

"Meanwhile, the witnesses laid their coats at the feet of a young man named Saul." (Acts 7:58)

This seems innocent enough, but a few sentences later we are told,

"And Saul approved of their killing him." (Acts 8:1)

We can't be absolutely clear whether Saul was directly involved in the death of Stephen, joining the frenzied blood-lust of the crowd in the actual stoning, but what is certain is that Saul wanted it to happen and encouraged it. If Stephen's blood wasn't actually on Saul's hands, it was certainly on his soul and it seemed to inspire him to take his campaign against the Followers of the Way to a whole new level.

"Meanwhile, Saul was still breathing out murderous threats against the Lord's disciples. He went to the high priest and asked him for letters to the synagogues in Damascus, so that if he found any there who belonged to the Way, whether men or women, he might take them as prisoners to Jerusalem." (Acts 9:1-2)

The Saul we now see is passionate, focused, dedicated, determined and missional in his zealous pursuit of the cause that burns within his heart. But this wasn't just blind rage or vengeful bigotry, these actions came out of a heart captivated by a cause, a way of life, a relentless belief in the truths and ideals long held by this young man. These aren't the random ravings of some misled extremist, rather these are the calculated actions of someone who believes they are called by God to defend the honour of His name. Later when writing to the church at Philippi, he listed his pre-Christ religious credentials and what an impressive CV it is:

"If someone else thinks they have reasons to put confidence in the flesh, I have more: circumcised on the eighth day, of the people of Israel, of the tribe of Benjamin, a Hebrew of Hebrews; in regard to the law, a Pharisee; as for zeal persecuting the Church; as for righteousness based on the law, faultless." (Philippians 3:4-6)

Even without understanding the details of what Paul is referring to, it sounds impressive, right? And it was! Saul wasn't messing about, he was doing what he believed in and he wasn't going to be accused of doing a half-baked job. Saul was an all or nothing sort of person and within the box of his religious world, he pushed himself to the very edge of its boundaries. Within a very short time, every Follower of the Way probably knew who Saul was, what he was up to and that he wasn't likely to slow down until every disciple of Jesus was either scattered or stopped! Saul's cause was his box!

All of that changed one day as Saul journeyed to Damascus. On that road he had a life-changing encounter with the Jesus he was trying to destroy. He got up from the ground blind and dazed, made his way to a house in Damascus, and waited. Three days later, Ananias, a Follower of the Way reluctantly arrived to help him, having been told by God that Saul was God's "...chosen instrument to carry My name before the Gentiles and their kings and before the people of Israel..." (Acts 9:15). The rest, as they say, is history. Later when Paul was telling the story of how he encountered Christ, he declared to King Agrippa,

"I was not disobedient to the vision from heaven." (Acts 26:19)

The Paul we now see in the second half of the book of Acts is passionate, focused, dedicated, determined and missional in his zealous pursuit of the cause that burns within his heart. Paul's cause is his box – but now it's a new box. Instead of destroying the Church, he's helping to build it and spread it. Instead of running from Jesus, he's working for Him. Instead of seeking to extinguish the light, he's now carrying it to the ends of his world. I love what Allen says about Paul's box,

"In little more than ten years St Paul established the Church in four provinces of the Empire, Galatia, Macedonia, Achaia and Asia. Before AD47 there were no churches in these provinces; in AD57 St Paul could speak as if his work there was done, and could plan extensive tours into the Far West without anxiety lest the churches which he had founded might perish in his absence for want of his guidance and support."[1]

Note that he, "...could speak as if his work there was done...". On the road to Damascus, Saul was not only "saved from his sin", but he was dramatically transferred from one cause-box to another! Jesus smashed the religious cause-box that Saul was in and placed him in the cause-box of the Church. Sometimes we think that Saul was set free on the road to Damascus, but the truth is he was unbound and rebound. In truth, he was released from one box to serve in a greater, bigger and better box.

I believe Paul understood this, captured for us in his words to the church at Philippi:

"Not that I have already obtained all this, or have already arrived at my goal, but I press on to take hold of that for which Christ Jesus took hold of me." (Philippians 3:12)

Paul took hold of that for which he had been taken hold of! There is a lovely play on the same word in this statement. katalambánō meaning "to take hold" is used twice here. The first time Paul uses it of himself: "...but I press on to take hold of that...". The tense used here is aorist active subjunctive. Paul is seeking to attain and take hold of this thing. A literal translation might read, "if indeed I may lay hold of". There is no confusion over what Paul is seeking to take hold of, for his statement suggests single-minded determination and focus. Paul's goal is to take hold of what is before him. But what is before him?

"...for which Christ Jesus took hold of me."

The tense here is aorist passive indicative, pointing to an action that has taken place; a once-for-all action that has happened to Paul. He has been taken hold of and in turn he wants to take hold of that for which he has been taken hold of. On the road to Damascus, Jesus didn't just redeem a person, He redeemed a purpose and He didn't just save Saul from something, rather He saved him for something.

Paul declares in Philippians, "I know what I've been taken hold of for and therefore I am going to relentlessly, zealously and passionately pursue this thing in my life." He even refers back to his fantastic CV, mentioned earlier in the chapter, and informs us that for the greatness of this new cause-box which he's discovered, he is prepared to let go of anything that doesn't fit the cause in order to take hold of the cause.

"But whatever were gains to me I now consider loss for the sake of Christ. What is more, I consider everything a loss because of the surpassing worth of knowing Christ Jesus my Lord, for whose sake I have lost all things. I consider them garbage, that I may gain Christ and be found in Him..." (Philippians 3:7-9)

Note two dramatic things from this statement:

The first is the fact that Paul uses the word "consider" three times. The word is hēgéomai and carries the idea of "leading out before the mind". It means to lead, go before, go first or lead the way. Paul parades the argument before himself and makes a clear and definitive call. His conclusion on what is important and what is not, does not reveal an emotional whim, or a reaction to an extreme event. Paul weighs it all up, looks at the cause, and considers that whatever cost he has to pay, it is worth it!

The second thing to notice is how Paul evaluates his previous box and the CV that went with it, describing it as "garbage" (NIV). The word is skúbalon and refers to useless, undesirable waste that can be thrown out. It can refer to waste fit for dogs, dung and even excrement. Paul's learning and background and upbringing of course was not "excrement" – in a certain cause-box this would have been regarded as gold. But rather Paul is saying that having understood that which Christ took hold of him for, having weighed everything up and considered it, what he had is like excrement in comparison to what he received. Whatever he lost in taking hold of Christ's purpose was nothing when compared to the pay off he was now enjoying. Paul realised that on the road to Damascus, he was lifted from one box and put into another. So instead of fighting it, he embraced it!

What do we learn from Paul's box-swapping experience?

1. Freedom is life in a God-box

The danger is that we think Paul's Damascus conversion was the moment he was set free, when in reality it was the moment he was rebound. Paul gloriously declares to the church at Galatia,

"It is for freedom that Christ has set us free..." (Galatians 5:1) and if we are not careful we can make this a mantra that allows us to think we are now in charge and, having been released from the slavery of sin, we are now free to do what we please and live how we want, provided we stay on the right side of moral and legal. But in the same book Paul talks of being "set apart from birth and called by grace" (1:15) and later urges the followers of Jesus to "live by the Spirit" (5:16); to allow ourselves to be "led by the Spirit" (5:18) and to "keep in step with the Spirit" (5:25). It seems our freedom is dependent on our walking in line with God's ways and keeping within the boundaries of His desires for us. It seems we are not really free at all.

This is so important and lies at the heart of our understanding of what it means to be saved, part of God's called-out community. It's a staggering thought, but the word "Church" as we use it, doesn't actually appear in the New Testament. The word that we ultimately take the word Church from is ekklēsía, which simply means "called out".

At the heart of this called-out community is a dynamic confession, first spoken by Peter,

"You are the Christ, the Son of the Living God." (Matthew 16:16)

This is not just any old community of people, this is a community of people drawn together around one common confession: that Jesus is the Christ. That means He is at the centre of this community and therefore if the community is to function, it can only do so in Him, by Him and from Him. I cannot be a part of this community and have my own confession or my own "sub-culture" or be my own boss. If I want to truly be part of this community, then I must submit to the Head of it and allow His way to become mine. Too many "join" the Church but want to remain their own boss, live their own way and enjoy their so-called religious freedoms. But this thinking is fundamentally flawed.

The Church, the Jesus Community, is one that has been called by God.

We cannot enter the Church because we want to. We enter into it because He wants to! The Church is not an institution we join, rather it is a community to which we are called. Being part of the Church is not primarily about us, it's about Him and we cannot enter it without a supernatural call, without (as Paul experienced) the realignment of our lives from one cause-box, to the greatest cause-box. But let us not be misled, God is not calling us to be free to do what we want. Rather He is calling us to be free to do what He wants!

The Church, the Jesus Community is one that has been called to God. Paul grasped this from the very beginning, maybe because of his Jewish roots. Having lived in a called-out community with the great Shema confession at its core, Paul understood that the key to truly embracing this community was the truth that God was at the centre and everyone and everything else was submitted to that truth. Paul was well versed in the glorious confession that resounded at the heart of his world:

"Hear, O Israel: The Lord our God, the Lord is one. Love the Lord your God with all your heart and with all your soul and with all your strength." (Deuteronomy 6:4)

Look at it carefully. The individual is nowhere to be seen. This confession is not about what "I" want or what "I" need. This confession isn't about me coming to get something and feeling good about myself. This confession is about who God is and what He wants. This sits at the very heart of Paul's Jewish understanding and therefore it would have been relatively easy for him to transfer that reality into this new community, formed around the Christ Confession.

Too many see their freedom in terms of "what God will do for me" and of course we believe that God can do and will do amazing things for us. Too often we've allowed our individuality and specific needs to drive the worship agenda and make our great faith more about us than about Him. But if we are to live a life like Paul, in attitude at least, if not in action, then we must come to the freedom of worshipping God with all our being for who He is and seeking first and foremost what He wants above anything we might want.

Jesus put it magnificently when He said,

"But seek first His Kingdom and His righteousness and all these things will be given to you as well." (Matthew 6:33)

The Church, the Jesus Community is one that has been called for God.

Writing to the called-out community in Corinth, Paul could not have been clearer when he said,

"And He died for all, that those who live should no longer live for themselves but for Him who died for them and was raised again." (2 Corinthians 5:15)

The ultimate evidence that we have been redeemed is that we not only celebrate what we have been saved from, but we take hold of that which we have been saved for. We haven't just been bought out of the slave market of sin, but we have been bought to the purpose of God. This verse echoes Paul's own experience, where on that Damascus road he moved from living for himself (even though he thought he was living for God) to living for God Himself. Like Paul, we must grasp and strive to take hold of the "for" of God's redemptive plan, not just the "from" of that plan. Paul's zeal, passion and influence came out of the reality that he understood both dynamic dimensions. He had been rescued and repurposed!

2. Poo or purpose?

Imagine being offered the stark choice of a briefcase full of money – more money than you ever dreamed of – and a carrier bag full of excrement. Seriously, what would you choose? Now if you hesitated for even a split second, I'm thinking you need to get out more! It's a crazy offer, I know, and in truth it's not a real choice at all, but nonetheless, that's the image Paul has given us in his comments to the Philippians. Look at his words again:

"...I consider them garbage, that I may gain Christ and be found in Him..."

Garbage or Christ? Excrement or opportunity? Poo or purpose? When it's put in such stark terms, it seems like a no-brainer, but yet at the heart of it is a real choice.

In the context of Paul's world, his garbage would have been the envy of many, representing the top of the ladder of success. Many in his old world would probably have been of the opinion that Paul had let go of gold to take hold of poo, but the irony remains that Paul sees it as the exact opposite. Paul considered, considered again and then reconsidered the claims of Christ's box and then wholeheartedly decided to step into it and make God's cause-box his world. Whatever he gave up and whatever he "lost", he decided it was worth it.

At moments like this we tend to use words like sacrifice, but I believe Paul thought more in terms of investment. He wasn't so much giving up, rather he was giving in. Jesus told the story of a man who discovered some treasure buried in a field. Jesus said the man immediately went and sold everything he had in order to buy the field so that in turn, he could have the treasure. Whatever the cost, he had to have the field. He knew in the light of the value of the treasure that the cost was an incredible investment, not a sacrifice (Matthew 13:44). In 1948, while at Bible College, a young man wrote these now immortal words in his journal; words that he would ultimately express through his own martyrdom:

"He is no fool who gives what he cannot keep, to gain that which he cannot lose."[2]

The dictionary defines sacrifice as,

"The giving up of something for the sake of something else."

It defines invest as,

"To spend (money, time etc.) on something with the expectation of profit."

Both words imply, and in fact demand, cost, but the mentality which governs both actions are poles apart. A sacrifice mentality can often be one dominated by loss-cost. Whereas an investment mentality is one motivated by return-cost. Both give away and both make contributions, but one expects no return and therefore potentially sees any contribution as a loss, whereas the other expects a return in some capacity and therefore sees the cost as an investment.

Paul knew that whatever he gave up was a bargain in comparison to all that he would get back in and through Christ Jesus. His sacrifice (if it was that) was worth it and his investment was the wisest he ever made, giving him returns beyond his wildest dreams.

What do you want? The poo of your own apparent freedom or the purpose-box; the great cause-box that God offers you today?

3. To take hold you have to let go

The final lesson Paul teaches us from these immense words is simple yet profound. If we want to take hold of that for which Christ has taken hold of us, then we must be prepared to let go of what we're currently holding on to! The box of Paul's pre-Christ life was sizeable, at least in the context of that world, and to Paul it must have felt like he had reached the highest levels of his world. And yet, Jesus showed him another box, a bigger box, a box that would allow all the gifts and callings that the Almighty had placed within Paul in his mother's womb to take flight and touch the skies of God's greater purpose. In order to gain Christ and His cause-box, Paul had to be prepared to let go of everything he knew and all that he had. Being prepared to let go of one, granted him the opportunity to embrace the other.

The cry of our world is "I want to be free ... I want to be able to do what I want..." But the truth is, no matter who you are, such an aspiration is impossible. Even if our world thinks it is free, its people operate within the boundaries of philosophical, cultural, religious, gender, ethnic and financial boxes. True personal freedom is a myth, an idea that exists more in the hearts of fallen humankind than in the mind of God. Even in Eden, God's garden of delights and His first blueprint for our world, our first parents were free only when they stayed within the boundaries set out by God. Within those boundaries, within the box of that magnificent garden, they were naked and without shame; they had an unbroken relationship with God and their work was productive and fulfilling. They lived in the freedom of God-centric worship, God-created worth and God-commanded work, but all within the box of a garden and under the guardianship of God's word. When they listened to the lie of the serpent, their break for freedom only left them in a smaller, poorer box.

On 15th August 1961, Conrad Schumann got his fifteen minutes of fame when he decided to do the unthinkable. As a young East German soldier he was guarding the site that was to become the infamous Berlin Wall. For the next thirty years the wall would stand as a symbol of the cold war generation and the gulf in ideologies between two opposing forces. Sadly it also divided families, friends and a nation. I don't know exactly what was going through Conrad's mind at that moment he decided to jump to "freedom", a moment immortalised by a fortuitously placed photographer, but I know this: he made a decision to leave all that he had and all that he knew to embrace what he believed would be a better opportunity. Conrad let go and took hold!

What are you holding on to? What freedom-myth are you

grasping at which ironically prevents you from taking hold of the greatest freedom of all? Don't be fooled into thinking that if you're not in God's box you're free. True freedom can only be experienced when we surrender all we are and have to the Christ, the Son of the Living God. The great Apostle simply exchanged one box for another; he moved from a man-made box to the box God designed for him before the foundations of the world were made. We admire Paul's achievements in church planting and the contribution he makes to our New Testament, but at the heart of this incredible man was a considered choice: on the road to Damascus he climbed into God's box and never climbed out!

Summary and Reflections

"Sometimes we think that Saul was set free on the road to Damascus, but the truth is he was unbound and rebound... he was released from one box to serve in a greater, bigger and better box!"

1. Freedom is life in a God-box

"... our freedom is dependent on our walking in line with God's ways and keeping within the boundaries of His desires for us."

We are called *by God*

"We cannot enter the Church because we want to; we enter into it because He wants to! "

We translate the word ekklēsía as Church, but it really strictly means 'called out community'. *How might this truth change the way we think about 'how' we became a Christian?*

We are called *to God*

"... this confession (Shema) is about who God is, and what He wants."

In what way does the God-centric nature of this faith community challenge who and what we focus on?

We are called *for God*

"We haven't just been bought out of the slave market of sin, but we have been bought to the purpose of God. "

How might our understanding of redemption be transformed if we grasped the language of "for" as well as "from"?

2. Poo or Purpose?

"He (Paul) wasn't so much giving up rather he was giving in."

If we moved from (giving up) sacrifice to (giving in) investment, how might that switch in emphasis change our current thinking, confession and conduct?

3. To take hold you have to let go

"Being prepared to let go of one, granted him the opportunity to embrace the other."

Is there anything you are holding on to that you think is preserving your freedom, but is actually restricting your freedom in God? What is preventing you from taking hold of that for which Christ took hold of you?

Footnotes:

1. Allen, R., Missionary Methods, St Paul's and Ours, (USA: World Dominion Press, 1962), p.3.

2. Jim Elliot

4
ONE THING AND EVERYTHING

It is ironic that in the very same letter where Paul categorically states that he is taking hold of the "one thing" for which Christ Jesus took hold of him, that we get a statement from him that seems to suggest the complete opposite.

"I can do everything through Him who gives me strength." (Philippians 4:13)

How often have we heard this quoted in services in an attempt to inspire us to press forward in Jesus, to inspire us to do more and be more? Yet within the letter to the saints at Philippi, it offers an apparent contradiction within Paul's thinking. Earlier, Paul was clear that Jesus had apprehended him and his reaction suggests that Paul is pretty certain as to why he has been apprehended and what that looks like. Paul's laser focus comes through in phrases like "I consider", "press on", "one thing" and "win the prize" and yet, as he draws the letter to a close, he seems to be offering us a blank cheque of possibility and opportunity, that any of us can do anything we want to do in Christ.

The statement found in verse 13 literally reads, "All things I am strong for in the (One) strengthening me." The key is in understanding what Paul means by "all things" or "everything" and the clue for this is in the context of the statement itself.

When I was in Sunday school, we were taught that a text taken out of context can often become a pretext, and if ever that little maxim held true it's around this verse, which I think might rate in the top five of Paul's most misquoted statements.

In the verses proceeding, Paul expresses his gratitude for the Philippians for renewing their concern for him. Having helped him in the past (Philippians 4:15), Paul is thankful that their generosity and support to him is once again swinging into action. However, he doesn't want to be a burden to them and so explains how he has coped with the financial and economic challenges he's faced in sharing the Gospel. His explanation carries three key elements that, when broken down, form a powerful insight into Paul himself and how he addressed life within his box.

Learning

Twice Paul says,

"... I have learned to be content whatever the circumstances" (v 11).

"I have learned the secret of being content in any and every situation..." (v 12).

On the surface of it these statements look the same, but they are subtly different and it's worth noting the differences.

In verse 11 Paul says, "I have learned...". The word he uses here is *manthánō* and points to the normal or usual process of learning. Having been given some information such as 2+2=4, I "learn something", or having gone through an experience of putting my hand in the fire and realising it burns and hurts, I "learn something". Paul, however, doesn't seem to be pointing to a single moment of learning, rather to ongoing learning that draws upon the collective experiences throughout his life up to this point. Through his many trials, travels and triumphs, Paul has been actively *learning* how to be content, and so can confidently proclaim to the church at Philippi that whether they help him or not, he will remain strong and secure in who he is and what he knows.

In verse 12 Paul says, "I have learned the secret...". The word used here is *memyēmai* and is different from that used in verse 11. In fact, this is the only time this word is used in this specific way in the whole of the New Testament. The idea implied here is not so much learning something in a conventional way, but rather learning it by *reception* – receiving a mystery or getting something you didn't learn! We might want to use words like "revelation" when thinking of this type of learning; the moment when the penny drops, when our eyes are opened, when the light comes on – you know, the clicking moment.

When I was eight years old, I was sitting in a children's service in a City Mission in Belfast. The man at the front was teaching us from Revelation 3:20: "Behold I stand at the door and knock..." I have since learned that those words weren't actually directed to non-believers, but to followers of Jesus and the way the preacher used them that night was not strictly correct ... yet, the Holy Spirit took those words and in an instant, I saw Jesus the Son of God, standing at the door of my "heart", knocking and asking to come in.

Immediately, even as an eight-year-old, I knew two things – firstly, Jesus Christ was the Son of God and secondly, I needed to let Him into my life. I turned to my friend and said, "Tonight I'm going to become a Christian." Now, I did not learn that information in a classroom, but that night I learned a secret. I learned it by revelation. I got some information from God which would change me forever. This is the same idea as seen in Matthew 16, when Peter confesses that Jesus is the Christ and Jesus informs him that Peter didn't get this by human learning, "...but by My Father in heaven..." (Matthew 16:13-20).

In making his case to the church at Philippi, Paul demonstrates to them that he has learned in two powerful ways, firstly by information and secondly by impartation. These two very different ways to learn are not in competition, but rather are working together to produce a powerful, resilient man, who is able to do the things God has asked of him. Paul is able to relentlessly take hold of the thing for which Christ has taken hold of him, because he has learned and continues to learn both by information and impartation.

But note what Paul has learned. He has learned to be *content*. The word is *autárkēs*, meaning literally "self-sufficient". This may sound out of step with the passage, and with Paul himself, and you'd be right. But it's not pointing to self-sufficiency in a proud or arrogant sense, but rather with the idea that one has enough, one is sufficient, full and adequate; one is satisfied with one's lot.

In the context this speaks powerfully to us. Paul is neither arrogantly self-sufficient nor, at the other extreme, putting up with mediocrity. He is content. He has come to understand what his box looks like, what it requires, what it costs and, at times, what it feels like.

He has learned to stay within the boundaries that God has set for him and to work and live within the limits that God's purpose demands of him. He has come to a place of "this is enough for me ... it is sufficient."

Knowing

Twice in verse 12 Paul says,

"I know what it is to be in need..."

"I know what it is to have plenty..."

The word used here, *oída,* is identical in every way in both statements and Paul repeats the idea that he has come to know. This knowing is via experiences of plenty and want; too much and not enough. The great apostle has come to know what it is like to have his pantry overflow with goodies and his belly rumble in hunger.

It is interesting, however, that his two declarations of knowing are sandwiched by the two statements of learning. Paul's knowing and learning are connected. He hasn't just learned the theory of contentment, but he has come to know the outworking of this learning, whether by information or impartation, in the sharp reality of every day living. Paul is not merely "selling" the product, he owns the product. He's not telling Philippi how to do it, he's showing them!

Learning (regardless of how powerful and lofty), only becomes reality in knowing. When we know it in the everyday, it's a sign we've truly learned it. If we can still keep God at the centre when our cup overflows with goodness, and if we can keep our mouth from cursing when we're down to our last crumb of bread, then our learning has truly become knowing. It's easy to sit in a lovely building listening to a preacher or leader unpack the Bible and say amen at the appropriate sacred moments. It's another thing entirely to be living Amen when life sucks, when the lights have gone out and the worship band has gone home. Paul learned to be content. How do we know? Because he lived content in the midst of extremes of plenty and need. His knowing proved his learning to be truth, powerful and authentic!

Doing

In verse 13 Paul concludes,

"I can do everything..."

When we connect the statement in verse 13 to those in 10, 11 & 12, the force and focus of everything starts to change. It seems that everything in verse 13 relates back directly to the reference to "any and every situation" in verse 12. For me the conclusion of verse 13 is obvious and liberating. Paul isn't saying I can do *everything*, as in *anything*, rather he is saying, I can do "all these things". In other words, I can do the things I've learned in the context of taking hold of that for which Christ took hold of me.[1] When we put it all together something very powerful starts to emerge.

Paul swaps his box for God's box:

"...I press on to take hold of that for which Christ Jesus took hold of me..." (Philippians 3:12)

Paul focuses on God's purpose for his life:

"I press on towards the goal to win the prize for which God has called me heavenwards in Christ Jesus." (Philippians 3:14)

Paul learns contentment by information and impartation in pursuit of the prize:

"I have learned to be content ... I have learned the secret of being content..." (Philippians 4:11-12)

Paul knows his learning in the crucible of his call:

"I know what it is to be in need ... I know what it is to have plenty..." (Philippians 4:12)

Paul has the strength through Jesus to do "all these things":

"I can do everything [my "everything"] through Him who gives me strength." (Philippians 4:13)

To summarise all this:

Paul is only able to do "everything" that sits within the "one thing"!

So what does this mean to us as we seek to go beyond by staying within?

1. Everything doesn't mean everything

I remember once hearing a preacher say something regarding this verse. He said, "I've looked at the Greek for everything and discovered it means 'everything'." Oops! Clearly Paul did not mean everything in the sense of "anything" in this verse. In fact, the true meaning is at the opposite end of this thinking. Paul is telling us that we actually cannot do everything, because everything here doesn't mean everything. Rather it points to the things that God requires of us and asks for us.

If we live in the world of everything, then we're setting ourselves up for almost continuous disappointment with God and life. The thought that you and I can just do what we want because we slap the phrase "through Jesus who gives me strength" on the end is not only naïve, but a presumptuous way of regarding God. That's when people write cheques God never promised to cash, or when we try stuff that God never told us to do, or when we claim things that God never wanted us to have.

I realise this may sound terribly negative to some, especially for those coming from a Spirit-filled Pentecostal tradition who believe in the exploits of the Church in the book of Acts. But it's not meant to be. I don't want to restrict you, I want to release you. I don't want to see you waste time and energy on fantasies, I want your life to be energised by divine vision. I don't want you to climb a ladder, only to discover it was leaning against the wrong wall, rather I want you to get to the end of your life and know you ran the right race and you lived the right life.

No doubt some will reject my appeal on the basis of small thinking and negative confession, but nothing could be further from the truth. Paul didn't go everywhere, he didn't do everything and he didn't try to be everyone. The reason we remember Paul was because he had the courage to stick with the "one thing", be the person God made him and stay within the boundaries God set for him. He was content with this and as a result God took him higher and further than he could have dreamed.

Everything doesn't mean everything ... but it does mean something!

2. Your "everything" is linked to your "one thing"

There is an "everything" you can do (not good English, I know) and there are "all things" that are perfectly possible for you. However, the Bible teaches us they can only reside within the boundaries of God's "one thing".

There's a beautiful story in Luke 7, when a Roman Centurion made an approach to Jesus for the welfare of his servant. The fact that the Centurion "valued his servant highly", made an approach to Jesus through some Jewish elders, was respected by the people his army were oppressing, and built a local synagogue, should give us a clue that this man was no ordinary soldier. Clearly more was going on. However, as remarkable as all that is, I don't think it's the most remarkable fact about this man. On asking Jesus to heal his servant, the Centurion speaks (through the Jewish elders which means these words were intentional), and says,

"For I myself am a man under authority, with soldiers under me. I tell this one 'Go', and he goes, and that one 'Come', and he comes. I say to my servant, 'Do this', and he does it." (Luke 7:8)

Two things here are worthy of note:

Firstly, the Centurion understood that to have authority, one had to be under it.

He knew that if he stepped out of line or over his boundary, he would not be able to exercise any authority over any other person under his command. The only reason he was obeyed was because he was being obedient, living within the boundary of Roman authority. He had it because he was under it. He could do it, because he was under it.

Secondly, the Centurion recognised that Jesus was "under" authority.

Of course, he was also acknowledging that Jesus had authority, hence the request. But the Roman gets it. He understands how it works. In the same way that he gets to order people around because he is under authority, so Jesus is doing amazing things because He is under a "greater" authority. As an aside, I believe that the Roman is seeing Jesus as the Christ, the Messiah, and that's why Jesus is so blown away by his faith, declaring,

"I tell you, I have not found such great faith even in Israel." (Luke 7:9)

This can't be referring to faith for healing, because others have been healed before this moment. This has to be about something deeper, greater, more significant even than healing. This is about who Jesus is and how He works. Somehow, a Roman Centurion saw it, understood and connected to it. Jesus has authority because He's under God's authority. Jesus was God's anointed, His Messiah!

The Roman was right, of course, but oh how we miss this. We love the "command my servant to be healed" bit, but move quickly over the "under authority" bit. Jesus was able to do everything that was linked to God's one thing for His life. Outside of God's one thing, Jesus (in theory at least) had zero authority to work and act on God's behalf, doing God's work and bringing honour to God's name. Paul learned the same thing. He grasped that the only authority he had was that granted to him by God for the things that God wanted.

One thing that truly terrifies the devil and has the power to make a genuine difference in our world, are people living under and working out of God's authority. When we align with God, stay within His boundaries and do what only He has told us to do, we are invincible. We have an authority that can speak to mountains, sickness and impossibility and see it yield to God. The devil doesn't mind noise, bluster, words or clever techniques. What he fears the most is God-given authority, because he cannot withstand such a force.

Jesus knew it, Paul knew it, the Centurion knew it, and even the devil knows it. So why do we try to fight it and "command" beyond the boundaries of our authority? If we have the courage to stay within God's boundary, we'll always have His authority!

3. His strength is available for His thing

"All things I am strong for in the (One) strengthening me."

The logic is gloriously simple, yet transformationally profound. If Paul takes hold of God's one thing and stays within that boundary, then he can and will receive all that he needs to do that one thing. In fact, Paul can expect to receive everything he needs to get the job done. Paul was able to draw on that well of supernatural strength to do the most amazing things. The man's work rate is breathtaking and the reach and impact he achieves with his team still stands as an example of what can be done by those truly dedicated to the cause.

If we are prepared to use the car for the right journeys and drive it in the right direction, carrying the right passengers and using it for the purpose for which it was designed, then God is committed to filling the tank with fuel to ensure we can get to where He wants us to go and do what He wants us to do. When Jesus was about to leave His young followers, He urged them to stay in Jerusalem and "...wait for the gift my Father promised..." (Acts 1:4). That sounds wonderful, but the purpose of the power was revealed just a few seconds later when Jesus reminded them,

"But you will receive power when the Holy Spirit comes on you; and you will be my witnesses in Jerusalem, and in all Judea and Samaria, and to the ends of the earth." (Acts 1:8)

But here's the thing, you only need the power if you're going to engage in the purpose! If the car is going to sit on the driveway every day looking pretty, then it doesn't need fuel. Not only has God promised us strength and power in Christ and through the person of the Holy Spirit, but His strength and power is only for His stuff, not for ours. He will not allow His power to be used for our personal gain and glory.

The story of Samson is an amazing one. Contained in

Judges 13-16 it's well worth a read. Though his beginnings are supernatural, his first recorded words are a clue as to what comes next:

"I have seen a Philistine woman in Timnah; now get her for me as my wife." (Judges 14:2)

This pattern pretty much follows throughout the whole episode. Samson does mostly Samson stuff and God's Spirit shows up on a number of occasions to get His deliverer out of trouble. Samson had gift and strength, but the story shows that he used it consistently for the wrong stuff and too often for selfish ends. Samson was a boy in a man's body and he believed that God would keep showing up to help him. But of course, one day while lying in the lap of a beautiful woman, Samson gave away the secret to his strength.

Once shaved and bound, Delilah called out to Samson to see if he could break out as he had done before. As Samson awoke, he reasoned in his head,

"I'll go out as before and shake myself free."

But then the Bible adds a terrifying comment:

"But he did not know that the Lord had left him." (Judges 16:20)

It's too simplistic to think that Samson's strength left solely because his hair was shaved, although this is in the text (16:19). I truly believe it left because God left – and God left because Samson kept climbing out of his God-shaped box to do his own thing.

Some of us, of course, know the end of the story. Not only does his hair grow again, but sense and spirituality return to the man who should have been much more than he now was. In one final act of defiance, Samson prayed between the pillars.

"O Sovereign Lord, remember me. O God, please strengthen me just once more ... Let me die with the Philistines." (Judges 16:28-30).

Possibly for the first time in his life, Samson was where he was supposed to be. I don't mean between the pillars, but in the place were God wanted him: a place of surrender, humility and death. His greatest feat was his last, and his most enduring impact came when he finally stopped trying to use his God-given gifts, strength and fuel for his own ends and completely submitted them to God. I truly believe, had Samson died sooner, he would have lived longer!

The strength that Jesus offers is only for the stuff that He endorses. If we want to run off and do a million things He doesn't want us to do, then we have to find a way to fund and fuel that by ourselves. However, if we have the courage to stay within the boundaries He has set, stick to the one thing of His purpose for us, then He is obligated to fill our tank and give us the strength we need to do the thing He wants.

Listen to Paul, the Centurion, Samson and the Master... the everything of anything is a myth that God won't support or fuel. However, the everything of one thing is actually what God wants and if we have the courage to stick with the one thing, then His everything is possible.

Summary and Reflections

"Paul is only able to do 'everything' that sits within the 'one thing'!"

1. Everything doesn't mean everything

"If we live in the world of everything, then we're setting ourselves up for almost continuous disappointment with God and life."

What might be the repercussions of trying to do "everything"?

2. Your everything is linked to your one thing

"... there are 'all things' that are perfectly possible for you."

The Centurion understood that he could only do the "everything" granted to him by the authority he was under. It was the authority boundary that created his opportunity.

List the thing(s) that as a follower of Jesus you believe you have true God-given authority to do.

3. His strength is available for His thing

"All things I am strong for in the (One) strengthening me."

Paul can expect from God all that he needs to do the everything within the one thing.

Go to the previous list above you've just made. *What strength (gifts, opportunities, abilities, resources etc) has God already given you for those things? Do you have the strength for those areas?*

"The strength that Jesus offers is only for the stuff that He endorses."

Footnotes:

1. "Everything" in v13, πάντα, seems to link clearly to "in everything" and "in all things", ἐν παντὶ, καὶ ἐν πᾶσιν, in v12.

5
YES AND NO

❖

In December 2008 the movie *Yes Man* was released and went straight to No.1 at the box office during its first week. In the movie, bank loan officer Carl Allen (played by Jim Carrey) becomes increasingly withdrawn from his friends since his divorce from his wife, Stephanie, and gets talked into going to a "Yes" seminar. Whilst there, he meets motivational guru Terrance Bundley, who forces (sorry, motivates) Carl into making a public agreement with him that he will no longer be a "no man". From that moment on he will say "yes" to every opportunity and request that comes his way. As you can imagine, mayhem ensues with a range of weird, morally questionable, awful and sometimes heart warming experiences. Locking into saying "yes" created for Carl a world of unpredictable scenarios where almost anything could happen.

Most people find it easier to say yes than no, and as a result find themselves living to the beat of someone else's drum. Of course it is a good thing to be generous and kind with our time, talents and resources. Saying yes to things that positively impact those around us always makes us feel good. But nonetheless, we have to face the challenge of a world that always seems to be asking for something. If we decide to live like Carl, then our lives will certainly be exciting, but they'll also be chaotic, random and, at the end of the day, seriously depleted. I'm not suggesting that you or any of your friends would be foolish enough to say "yes to everything", but I meet many people who are saying yes far too often – and to things and people they've no reason to say yes to.

When Jesus hung on the cross He spoke out seven statements, the penultimate one of which was "It is finished" (John 19:30). But what was finished? At a macro level, Jesus had paid for the sins of the world, becoming God's sacrificial lamb, taking upon Himself the wrath of God for all humankind. But at a more personal level, Jesus had actually finished the unique task that the Father had asked of Him. He had stuck to the course set out for Him. He had kept His eyes fixed on the goal before Him. He had resisted all temptation to deviate from His God-given path. Jesus finished because He said yes and no, all at the same time.

Let me illustrate this by looking at two dynamic passages of the Bible. Though at first they seem unconnected, I want to show you how closely linked they are, and the lessons we can draw from them.

The first is Philippians 2:5-11. Take the time now to pause and read this.

The second is John 13:1-17. Again, take the time to read this.

In Philippians 2, Paul gives us some magnificent Christology, demonstrating through theological truth that Jesus is our model of living within the context of Christian community. He desires that the "attitude" that Jesus manifests would be the very DNA of those who follow Him, showing the world what Jesus looks like through our attitudes and actions towards one another.

For me John 13 is the perfect "incarnation" or demonstration of everything contained in Philippians 2. If we read Philippians 2 and ask the question, "What does this look like practically?" I believe John 13 gives us a crystal clear answer.

The parallels between the two passages are striking. In both we have a descent.

In Philippians 2 Jesus starts as God, becomes a servant and then dies. In John 13 Jesus starts as "divine" Rabbi, becomes a servant and serves.

Then in both we have an ascent.

In Philippians 2 God intervenes and we have, therefore, exaltation and a name above every name. In John 13 we have Jesus robing, returning to His place and referring to Himself as Lord, the only time He does so in the whole of the Gospels.

Perhaps the diagram below will help visualise this.

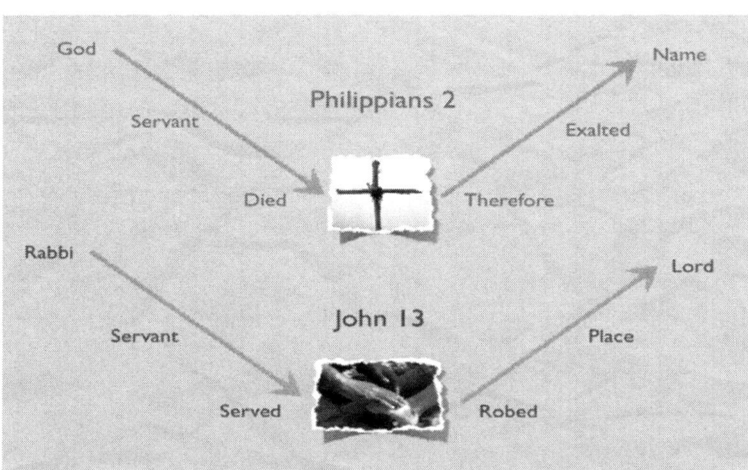

But none of this could happen without Jesus being able to say yes and no!

Let's go back to the Philippians 2 passage. Notice that in the *descent*, it is Jesus who is doing everything. For example, in verses 5-8 He doesn't grasp at being God, He makes Himself nothing, He takes the form of a servant, He humbles Himself and then He becomes obedient to death. In the *ascent* (verses 9-11), God the Father is doing everything for Jesus. God exalts Him to the highest place and gives Him a name above every name. We'll come back to this a little later in the chapter, but I want you to see that within the descent there are three incredible couplets that sit together.

1st Couplet – Identity and Security

"Who being in very nature God, did not consider equality with God something to be grasped..." (v6)

Before there was Jesus, there was God the Son. Jesus is the human embodiment of God the Son and therefore has a human beginning. But God the Son is the Eternal, All-knowing, All-Powerful, All-present Creator God, who was and is and ever shall be. Paul makes it clear who the Son is, but also that the Son knew who He was, and yet let go of who He was – with all associated rights, glory and privilege – to become "other", something else, in order to do the will of the Father. The Son becomes Jesus, knowing who He is, knowing He is God. Out of that profound sense of identity, He is secure enough to let go of His position to fulfill the purpose. He remains God, but willingly takes on a form that disguises who He is and makes Him unknowable for some, even though He came in human form to be known.

I love how the Message puts John 1:14:

"The Word became flesh and blood and moved into the neighbourhood..."

Jesus was able to move neighbourhoods because He knew who He was, and the clarity of His identity created such security that it allowed Him to take on a different form and move into a different world.

John 13 – what does that look like?

Identity

"Jesus knew that the Father had put all things under His power, and that He had come from God and was returning to God." (v3)

The pre-incarnate pattern continues in His human context. Jesus, as a man who learned the ways of God, knew who He was. Most of the young men settling down on their couches for supper think He is an outstanding Rabbi, but He knows He's more than that. He knows He is God the Son. He knows what authority He has and He knows where He has come from and where He is going. He knows who He is!

Security

"So He got up from the meal, took off His outer clothing and wrapped a towel around His waist... (v4)

It wasn't Jesus' "job" to wash the feet of His friends. Certainly, as the Teacher/Master of the group, this would not have been expected of Him, and in the absence of a servant, the duties would be the responsibility of the youngest to the oldest. As the oldest in the room and the Teacher of the group, Jesus was last in line for feet washing duties, yet He's first to rise and do what has to be done. In this action of rising and stooping, Jesus demonstrates immense security. Just as He was secure enough to leave heaven. Now, a few hours from His torturous execution, He rises from the place of honour and does the job that no Rabbi should have to do. He can do it because He is secure and He does it not because He has to, but because He wants to.

What do we learn from this couplet?

We learn that *clarity of identity will always produce security in purpose.*

When we know who we are it will always empower us to do whatever we need to do. With identity and security we will always be in pole position to say *yes* to what is great and *no* to what is good. Yes will become more than a word, it will become a lifestyle – and the more yes lives within us the easier it will be to say no to anything that sits beyond the boundary of our yes. God the Son was able to say no to heaven because He had said yes to earth. Jesus was able to say no to privilege because He had said yes to purpose.

Many say yes out of desperation to be liked and accepted, or in the hope that in doing so they will find their being. This is a tyrannous pathway that will always deplete us. When we discover our being, then our doing takes on a sharper focus, a greater meaning and a passionate intensity, which more often than not results in yes to great and no to good (or bad).

2nd Couplet – Choice and Authenticity

"...but made Himself nothing, taking the very nature of a servant..." (v7)

Note again, that God the Son is making the decisions here. None of this is being forced on Him, this is something He is doing willingly and freely. Flowing out of His identity and security, He is able to make difficult choices and take on an unusual form.

His difficult choice is captured in the words, "...but made Himself *nothing*...". There have been millions of words written around this one word, *kenóō,* translated here "made nothing", but which can also be translated "to make empty". In what sense Jesus made Himself empty has kept theologians (with much better and bigger brains than mine) occupied for years, so there is no way that we can come close to this issue in my little book. It is truly mysterious that God becomes flesh and somehow remains fully human and fully God. My heart gets this, though my brain overheats at any attempt to truly and fully understand it. Whatever empty means, we know two things for sure. Becoming empty for God the Son was a choice that He made willingly, and that His choice was costly, perhaps in ways that you and I as mere humans will never really be able understand.

However, if that wasn't enough, there's more! Not only does God the Son empty Himself and make Himself nothing, but He then takes something onto or into Himself, which is just as remarkable. Note the language: "...taking the very nature of a servant." The word used here by Paul is *morphḗ,* pointing to the form of something and in fact he uses the same word in the previous verse when speaking of God the Son being in "very nature God".

The play on words here is unmistakable. Paul declares that God the Son was in very nature and form God, but now has taken the very nature and form of a servant. In other words, Jesus isn't just serving He has become a servant. One can serve and not be a servant, but one cannot be a servant and not serve. Jesus, as God in flesh, is able to serve the purpose of God and say yes to Him because He has taken the very nature and form of a servant. Having done so, it is inevitable that He serves!

John 13 – what does that look like?

Choice

"After that He poured water into a basin and began to wash His disciples' feet..." (v5)

Jesus makes the choice, freely and personally to serve. He was within His rights to ask John (the youngest), to serve. But He did not. Rather, He made the choice to do it, not because He had to, but because He wanted to. Jesus chose to get up, fill the bowl and wash. This was a decision He was happy to make.

Authenticity

"...drying them with the towel that was wrapped around Him." (v5)

If you and I had walked in on that scene, not knowing who was who, we would have assumed that the guy washing the feet was either the youngest or a servant. Why? Because He looked like a servant – not only because of what He was doing, but because of how He looked. His state of "undress" and the fact that the towel was wrapped around Him was typical of any similar scene. Perhaps Jesus had witnessed this and observed as others had been "forced" to wash the feet because it was their job to do so. As we look on, we're shocked to discover that the guy with the towel is The Guy!

All this fits so perfectly with Paul's glorious Christology. Jesus served humanity in the macro context, because even though He had the nature of God, He put on and took in the nature of a servant. Now, at a micro level, in a room with a few of His closest friends, with no crowds, TV cameras or sound-bite opportunities, He washes their feet – not simply as their servant, but as The Servant. This is not an act or spin, this is the real deal. This is service from a servant!

What do we learn from this couplet?

We learn that *honest choices lead to authentic expression.*

Out of identity and security, God the Son made a conscious free choice to "do" and as a result produced something authentic and attractive.

On the night of that last supper, when others should have been serving Him, Jesus put aside all that He was entitled to and just served. That decision was an honest and free choice that flowed out of His identity and security, producing something so authentic and attractive that John had to find a place for it in his Gospel.

When our yes is a true, honest and free choice, it tends to produce something authentic. When our yes is due to pressure, guilt, fear or greed, it produces something that is real, but not necessarily authentic. We said yes because we had to, not because we truly wanted to!

3rd Couplet – Humility and Obedience

"...He humbled Himself and became obedient to death – even death on a cross!" (v8)

The images created by the word humble or humility tend to cause people varying levels of concern. As a young Christian growing up in Belfast, I was always concerned that humility would be taken as a license for a beating of some description. Images of doormats or weakness often fill our heads when we think of humility and in this context we might be tempted to do the same. In describing the humility of Jesus, Paul uses the word *tapeinóō*, which points to the idea of being made low or making oneself low, which is the context of our passage.

Let me try and illustrate the word with an image that might help. If you can, find a piece of A4 paper (go on, I'll wait). Hold it in front of you. Fold the paper in half. Now fold it again. Now, if you can, fold it again. Now, let me ask you a question. Is the folded paper in substance and constitution still an A4 sheet? (The answer is yes, just in case you're not sure). But what has happened to the paper? By folding it you've made it smaller. But have you made it lesser?

The piece of A4 paper in front of you is smaller but not less than it was. In fact, you have "humbled" the paper by folding it multiple times. But in making it smaller you have not diminished its size, just changed its appearance!

This is exactly the idea that I believe Paul is trying to get through to us. God the Son still exists. He's still in the "body of Jesus", but He's just smaller, not less than Himself. God the Son humbled Himself by letting go of His privileges and position, by taking the form of a servant and by making Himself smaller in order to fit the place that the Father wanted Him to go.

It follows then, that if God the Son humbled Himself, made Himself smaller for the Father's purpose, that the automatic outcome is obedience to the Father.

Obedience is the only possible outcome of genuine humility. Obedience is relatively easy, once our hearts are humbled; one naturally follows the other.

John 13 – what does that look like?

Humility

"He came to Simon Peter, who said to Him, 'Lord are you going to wash my feet?'" (v6-11)

Picture this. Jesus has taken the bold decision to serve His young friends. He comes to Peter and for some reason Peter decides to make a scene. The lad hasn't got the sense to shut up and let the Master work. Instead he tries to make a point. Maybe when we get to heaven, we can ask him what point he was trying to make. From verses 6-11 a conversation follows between Jesus and Peter. We could spend chapters on this conversation, but that's not where I want to go. Instead I want to point you to one simple fact.

While the conversation is going on, where is Jesus?

While Peter is rattling on, Jesus is patiently positioned at Peter's feet, waiting to wash them. Had Jesus been Celtic, by now Peter would have been wearing the bowl and chewing on the towel. But fortunately Jesus wasn't Irish! During this whole conversation Jesus is kneeling at Peter's feet. Think of the humiliation. It's bad enough that Jesus has to serve, but now while He's doing it, He has to wait while Peter makes up his mind as to whether or not he should join the party.

What grace, what control, what humility Jesus demonstrates. He could have stood up or moved on, but instead He makes the choice to remain where He is. Jesus was not humiliated at that moment, because He was in control. Rather, Jesus demonstrates the humility Paul expresses in Philippians 2. Jesus folds the paper to fit the moment ... and what a moment!

Obedience

"When He had finished washing their feet..." (v12)

Note this, it's so easy to miss: "When He had finished...". Jesus was obedient to the end and He was obedient to them all. The text seems to imply that Jesus must have washed Judas' feet that night too. Wow! Awkward moment for both men. But He did it nonetheless and perhaps in that moment He gives Judas one last chance to escape the clutches of Satan (but don't let that thought distract you from the rest of the chapter).

What do we learn from this couplet?

Obedience always flows from genuine humility. If, like Jesus, we are willing to make ourselves smaller (not lesser) for the purpose of God, if the yes we've signed up to truly lives within us, then obedience is the natural and irresistible outcome. So many wrestle with the dilemma of obedience when the real issue is the call to humility. If I know the yes God wants me to pursue, the issue is not whether I will obey it or not, but rather, if I'm prepared to alter my shape and size to fit into the purpose of the Father. If I can settle the humility question, the obedience question is also answered!

Yes, yes, yes!

Everyone needs a yes in their lives, but we must not and cannot go to the extremes of Carl, who ended up saying yes to everything. I believe we should be "yes people", but our yes must not be random, or driven by someone else's agenda. To live in the power of yes, it must come from the heart and live in the soul. If your yes is really someone else's yes, even though it might be a good yes, it will never truly fuel your soul nor fill your heart. Without your own yes, your life will be highjacked by somebody else's.

What are you saying yes to?

Why are you saying yes to this?

Who are you saying yes to?

Why are you saying yes to them?

These are questions worth asking.

When you say yes, no is a word of purpose not rebellion

I remind you of something I quoted earlier in the book. Warren Buffet said,

"The difference between successful people and very successful people, is that very successful people say no to almost everything."

We don't like the thought that Jesus said no to opportunities, people and possibilities, but the record of the Gospel clearly shows that He did. However, He did not say no in rebellion but in purpose. I submit to you that Jesus said no a lot, but you might not pick it up, because His no was in His yes.

The minute we say yes to anything, we're saying no to something else. If I say yes to my wife, I'm saying no to adultery. If I say yes to my children, I'm saying no to self-centred living. If I say yes to generosity, I'm saying no to greed.

When Jesus was asked which of the commandments were the greatest, He framed His answer in positive terms. On the basis of the confession as to who God is (The Shema), He summarised all the Law and the Prophets in two sentences by declaring that we should love God with our whole being and love our neighbour as ourselves. If we compare these two sentences to the Ten Commandments, we see the genius of Jesus turning a no into a yes.

Love God with your whole being equates to commands 1-4.

Love your neighbour as yourself, equates to commands 5-10.

If I love God and say yes to Him, then I'll automatically put Him first, honour His name and keep His ways.

If I love my neighbour and say yes to him/her, then I'll automatically treat them well. I won't steal from them, kill them, lie about them or to them, and I'll honour those within my world who deserve that honour.

In a moment of brilliance Jesus demonstrated that the Law was always meant to be about yes, not no!

No is another way of saying yes

Somebody once said that "concentration means elimination". I like that. I think this is what we see in Philippians 2 and John 13. Jesus is able to eliminate (say no) because He is concentrating (saying yes). Some people will try to tell you that no is just another word, but it's much more than that! No can be a statement of intent, an expression of clarity, a commitment to purpose and a keeper of the gate of your heart. No is an amazing word if used properly. There are some, of course, who only ever say no to everything. You've met them ... you know what I mean. I'm not talking about the no of narrow negativity, but rather the no of expansive purpose. When I say no, I'm actually saying yes!

Recently, I was invited to speak at a very exciting event. One of the organising team had heard me speak somewhere else and thought I would be "perfect" for their event. However, as I considered the invitation I realised they really wanted an Evangelist, and although I can and love preaching the message of an Evangelist, I'm not one! So, I let them know that this really wasn't me. I could do it; in my heart as a preacher I wanted to do it; but if I was honest I'd be saying yes to the wrong fit. So I said no and explained why. It would have been so tempting to say yes to the gig, but then I would have been saying yes to the wrong thing for the wrong reason, and that was likely to rob me of my authentic yes. In saying no to them, I was saying yes to purpose.

When Jesus said yes He was saying no, and when He said no He was saying yes.

When we say yes to God's box, we're also saying no to someone else (or even our own). When we're saying no to someone else's box, we're saying yes to His.

Live in the freedom of His yes and know the power of His no!

Summary and Reflections

"Most people find it easier to say yes than no, and as a result find themselves living to the beat of someone else's drum."

1st Couplet – Identity and Security

"... clarity of identity will always produce security in purpose."

2nd Couplet – Choice and Authenticity

"... honest choices lead to authentic expression."

3rd Couplet – Humility and Obedience

"Obedience always flows from genuine humility."

Yes, yes, yes!

"To live in the power of yes, it must come from the heart and live in the soul."

What are you saying yes to?

Why are you saying yes to it?
Who are you saying yes to?
Why are you saying yes to them?

When you say yes, no is a word of purpose not rebellion
"The minute we say yes to anything, we're saying no to something else."

Why do you find it so hard to say no to people?
With a clearer understanding of your purpose, what practicalities can help you to say no to the things that require your "no"?

No is another way of saying yes
"Concentration means elimination."
In what ways would the word "no" be transformed for you, if you saw it as part of yes?

"Live in the freedom of His yes and know the power of His no!"

6
THE PULL OF ANOTHER BOX

There are two types of boxes in life: those that restrict us and those that empower us. We have been talking about the latter. Every one of us will face challenging, negative restrictions that have been put on us by family, culture, background and our own mind set. I believe these boxes are designed to keep us small, ineffective and less than God meant us to be and must be addressed and dismantled, so that we can be truly free according to our shape and purpose. We must never give in to boxes of smallness, limitation and mediocrity that require of us only compromise and never courage. Too many live under the tyranny of other people's narrow expectations and a mindscape dominated by the idea of what we can't do rather than what we can do.

This book is not about restriction but liberation. It's not about excuses but empowerment. When we stay within the boundaries God has set for us, we'll always live in a large place and we'll always be and do more than we dreamed.

However, even when we know we're in the right box, when we know who we are and where God has placed us, and how best our gifts work, we are still faced with the temptation of "jumping boxes"; of leaving where we are for somewhere else; of believing that somehow, life beyond my God-given box is better and that God will understand that I need to have a look!

So what makes us jump boxes? What convinces us that life in someone else's box is better than our own and worth the risk of migration?

Crisis

When life is tough in your box it feels like everyone else on the planet is having a better time than you. In a struggling marriage, other people's partners can suddenly look attractive. In a difficult season at work, pulling the heads off chickens in a food factory can sound like a possible option (no offence to those who do). When your church is going through a rough patch, every message on Twitter and Facebook only seems to confirm the fact that your church sucks and everyone else's is rocking!

Crisis truly tests what we believe about the box we're in. When life is good, the box is lovely, but when life gets tough, our true attitudes about our context start to come out. We must be careful in moments of pain, discouragement or crisis, not to allow our emotions to drive our decisions, or else we will find ourselves planning our escape.

David was in a God-box. He was clearly set apart, called by God and anointed to be the next king of Israel. It all looked to be working out perfectly and when he was asked to serve the king in his court, God seemed to be opening the doors of opportunity. But as David grew, his king shrank and the inevitable happened.

Through his own insecurity, Saul felt threatened by the success of his servant and tried to kill him, forcing David into exile. While being pursued by Saul, David and his men hid in a cave. That same cave was the very one that the king would use to relieve himself during the pursuit. This was it – David's moment to take the king's life had come after all. God had surely handed Saul to him now.

But David refuses to jump boxes. He refuses to take what isn't yet his. He refuses to rise to the throne by blood instead of grace. David refuses to touch God's anointed and, to all intents and purposes, condemns himself to the box of exile and restriction. But if David was to be king, it would by God's hand, not his own. So David stayed in the box (1 Samuel 24). He refused to let crisis drive his agenda.

Sometimes we feel like we have to make things happen, force doors, win arguments and push down walls, and of course there are moments when God wants us to do that. But then there are other times when we know we are in the centre of His will and we have to let go of control, allowing Him to get us to where He wants us to go. As humans we struggle with this. We are all (to a lesser or greater extent) control freaks. Crisis, like few other things, will draw out the control freak in us. Resist! Stay where God has put you. Trust that the Lord who put you there, knows what you need and knows what comes next. Let your next move be by God's hand, not yours!

Coveting

I love my car. It's comfortable, efficient, practical, economical and fast when it needs to be. It gives me everything I need and it's paid for! However, recently I sat in a very, very nice, expensive, top of the range sort of car. You know, the ones with the cool badge that turns heads even though people try not to look. When I got back into my own car, suddenly it didn't seem so good. I heard noises that I hadn't noticed before, the clutch seemed a bit sticky and I have how many miles on the clock? There was, and is, nothing wrong with my car. It hadn't changed, I had!

The grass always looks greener in someone else's field, just ask Lot. He had it all. Lot had followed his uncle Abram to the land of promise and, as a result, became a wealthy man. So wealthy in fact that both his and Abram's herdsmen were clashing and they became convinced they could not remain together, even though the whole land lay before them. So a compromise was decided upon. Abram offered Lot a choice and the Bible says that Lot looked up and saw the whole plain of Jordan and it reminded him of the lush land he'd seen in Egypt. The text says, "So Lot chose for himself..." (Genesis 13:1-18). This is the statement at the heart of the story. Lot did not choose purpose, the call of God, or the greater good. Lot did not consult God, and remember how he became wealthy in the first place. No, Lot saw and chose for himself. He left the box of the land of promise for a land that would eventually negatively impact, destroy and corrupt his world.

When we covet, we invariably end up choosing for ourselves. When our eyes are inflamed by what seems good to us, our hearts will surely follow. It is so easy to covet someone else's world, church, car, marriage, kids, money and life, especially when we aren't so sure about our own. The danger with eyes that covet is that we always end up looking at the wrong stuff for the wrong reasons. That in turn will nearly always lead us to the wrong decision. Too many leave the God-box because of what they see, instead of trusting in what God sees!

Confidence

Confidence is a strange thing. Christians generally don't like talking about it unless it is connected to the Lord. But personal confidence flows out of an authentic confidence in the Lord. I'm pretty sure that when we are confident in Him, who He is and what He can do, that in turn impacts our own confidence to stand upon that solid Rock and live our lives well. My view of Him feeds directly into my view of myself. If He is my confidence, then I can live in confidence. But sometimes when it comes to the God-box we're in, we can face the challenge of both over-confidence and under-confidence.

When we're over-confident we think we can when we can't and therefore we think that the box we're in is a little too small for our super-duper abilities. So we leave our box to find a place that will more fully appreciate our skills and gifts. Of course, there are times when we "outgrow" a context, or perhaps the people we are with don't want to grow or go in the direction we do. That is part of life and it happens so often in many aspects of our journey.

But I'm not talking about that. I'm referring to an inflated view of our ability that believes we can be the Captain of 1,000, when really our gift is to be the Captain of 100. As Dr Laurence Peter suggested, "In a hierarchy every employee tends to rise to his level of incompetence." In other words, when we do well we get promoted, and when we do well, we get promoted again, until we eventually get promoted to a role we just can't do. Our confidence takes us to a place where our gifts cannot sustain us.

Confidence is good, but over-confidence can be bad. Believing we can when really we can't, may lead us to believe our own PR and cause us to rush to a box we're not equipped to live in.

Under-confidence can be just as destructive – when we think we can't but actually we can. How many times have people walked away from a job, a marriage or an opportunity, believing they could not, when everything within them and around them pointed to the fact that they could. Believing we can't do what God has asked us to do in the box in which He's placed us will cause many to migrate from their God-box to some other world. Under-confidence can be produced by a million things, but the result is always the same: we become convinced we cannot stay where we are because we cannot do what we're being asked. Remember, if God has placed you in that box, with those gifts and those skills, then you can. Even in the God-box there will always be things to learn, but when we are where we're supposed to be, we always have what we need and we can do what He is asking. Don't leave your God-box because you can't, when the One who put you there says you can!

Comparison

One of the hardest things in the world to do is to be you. Everyone believes they can just be themselves, but many of us don't want to admit that we're influenced by popularity, opportunity, company or comparisons. So many struggle with the simple reality of being true to ourselves. I have seen so much of this in the Church, even amongst leaders, where simple acceptance of self is often the hardest thing to do.

The hard taskmaster of comparison usually starts young, when we're compared to siblings, cousins or the lovely young man or woman next door. Industry and commerce often use the threat of peer success as a lever with which to get us to work harder, and even within the Church, one ministry, preacher, teacher or leader is compared to another, even though we're often comparing apples to oranges when we do so.

There is nothing wrong with modelling ourselves on an outstanding person or learning from them, this is truly biblical, but there is something fundamentally wrong when we want to be the same as them. Imitate the dynamic principles in and through which they live, but do it through the vehicle of your own God-shaped personality. Why do you want to be like the church down the road? Why are you comparing yourself to someone twenty years younger? Why do you make unhelpful and uneven comparisons of others when you know you are only putting an unbearable burden on them?

The world of comparison tends to produce certain offspring, namely those of *conformity* and *competition*. Conformity is that which is made in the image of others. Conformity always produces in us what others want to see. As a result it's usually not the image that God designed nor the person we're meant to be. When we conform to the wrong things for the wrong reasons we end up living in a grey, painful world where nothing of who we are ever surfaces and our creativity is stifled. We become stuck in a nowhere place; a non-person, doing nothing. This is existence not life, survival, not success. People in this world live lives of quiet desperation and painful frustration knowing that the person turning up to work today has already "left the building". No one wants to live in a world of conformity, yet millions do and come home every night to their beds emptier than when they left that morning.

The second child of comparison is *competition*. When we give in to comparison we end up fighting for all the wrong things against all the wrong people. Everyone is a threat and everything must be earned. There is nothing of grace or mercy. Rather, everything is smash and grab.

Healthy, proper competition is a good thing, but when we're competing for the crumbs on the floor, even when we win, we lose! When we live in the God-box, however, the call is not to competition, but excellence. We end up giving our best for Him, instead of trying to be better than someone else. We end up fighting for something that is great instead of fighting against something that, at best, is bad!

When we have a mind set that is always making unhelpful comparisons, we find ourselves not only looking over the edge of our box, but climbing the side and escaping. The beast of comparison can never be fully satisfied. When you feed it, it always wants more, and even when you give it your very soul, it won't be enough. Comparisons will distract you from who you are and convince you that you can be and must be someone else. The problem is, no matter how much you change, adapt and, dare I say it, evolve ... you'll always be you! God called you, helped shape you, gave gifts to you and believes in you. So stay in the box He made for you.

Compromise

Compromise is the "acceptance of standards that are lower than desirable". There are many influences that set the standards in the first place, but for us we're talking about something that is less than God designed and wants for our lives. If we know there is a God-box for us, and if we are aware of what that God-box is, then anything less than that is a compromise. We let go of what is more for less; we settle for good when great is the God-option.

One of the most tragic stories of this sort of compromise in the Bible is found in Genesis 25, where Esau abandons the box of his birthright for a bowl of stew. The story is fascinating and there is clearly a sub-text at work in the relationship between these twin brothers in a divided home.

Esau comes home starving after hunting. Jacob, his brother, just happens to be cooking at the time, which was lucky. Esau asks for some food and Jacob says, "Sure, if you'll sell me your birthright." The birthright in those days was everything. It essentially ensured that Esau was "number one" and would receive the lion's share of inheritance and authority from his father, Isaac. The lad was made! As you and I are reading, we're thinking that's a no-brainer. Esau will refuse and walk away. But no, in a staggering act of galactic stupidity, Esau sells his birthright to his young brother to get the stew, concluding, "What good is the birthright to me?" (Genesis 25:29-34). Esau left the box of promise for a bowl of stew because he had no comprehension of who he was, what he had and what it meant. He compromised and gained nothing.

That's the problem with this type of compromise – we end up with much less than we hoped for. We convince ourselves that nothing will change and that everything will be all right, but when we give away our identity, our call and our gifts, then nothing stays the same. Many truly believe it will all work out well in the end, despite such decisions, but it rarely does. God is good and gracious, but there's only so much even He can do for us when we're prepared to abandon the box He's designed for us. If the new box, the "better" box you're being offered, demands you are less than you, asks you to let go of your God-given dreams and beliefs, if you have to become something or someone else to get the prize on offer, turn it down. Stay where you are and live free!

Chance

It was Solomon who said,

"The race is not to the swift or the battle to the strong, nor does food come to the wise or wealth to the brilliant or favour to the learned; but time and chance happen to them all." (Ecclesiastes 9:11)

On first reading it looks as though Solomon is advocating the idea of luck or fate, but on closer inspection this is not the case. In essence he's saying that even when we do all the right things, we don't always get the right answer or outcome, and it looks like in the midst of all our planning, chance happens to each one of us. In other words, stuff just happens and we have to roll with it.

Sometimes we are tempted out of our box because a chance comes along that seems too good to miss – an opportunity we just must take. These are hard to resist and although we shouldn't look a "gift horse in the mouth", we need to make sure the horse is a gift and not a Trojan! Many have succumbed to what looked like the real thing – a great opportunity or a God moment – only to discover it wasn't. All that glitters isn't gold and just because we can, doesn't mean we should.

So how do I know if an opportunity is chance or call? Here are some questions that might help.

Does it fit with everything else God has said up to this point?

If what is being offered is suddenly radically different from everything you've done up to this point, or sounds different from everything God has said in your life, then at the very least, it might be worth pausing and assessing the situation. I know it looks good, but is it right? I believe that if the Lord is ordering your steps, then the next step shouldn't be a huge shock, even if it is a surprise. If the next step seems to be outside of the borders you've lived in, then you need to know with clarity if it is God.

Does it allow you to be the person He made you?

If the chance is offering an opportunity to truly be you, to bring out the best of who you are, then the chance might be the call of God. If it calls for you to be "someone else", behave in a different way or tone down who you are, then it's probably not God. We all have to learn, grow, adapt and develop, but you can't do that as yourself if "you" aren't welcome. Are they so desperate that any old "you" will do, or do they really want you?

Will it empower you to use the gifts He's given you?

Does the chance offer you the opportunity to not only use your gifts but further develop and grow them? Is what is being offered something anyone could do, or can only you do it? Your gifts are part of your personality and purpose. Not being able to use them will be like cutting away a part of you. You'll convince yourself (because the money is good, the area is great, the position is bigger and better, etc) that all those things will compensate for you not being able to work your gifts, but it won't. You may come home with a bigger pay-cheque, but you'll also have an empty heart. Ultimately, you'll have to decide which is more important!

If there were no money on the table, would you still do it?

This may seem a bit weird, but it will truly test your heart. Let's imagine they really wanted you, but there's no money. You'll have to work for free or get a part-time job to do it. Would you still do it? If you wouldn't do it for nothing, then you shouldn't do it at all. Money isn't a good enough reason to leave your God-box. Don't get me wrong, I like money and enjoy having it, but if we put purpose first, profit will follow. If we put profit first, purpose will invariably get lost on the journey.

Is this about ego or purpose?

In other words, is this about you or Him? If it's about you, then any chance will feel like a call – and even if it doesn't, you'll make the feeling fit. If it's about Him, then the call will always superimpose itself on the opportunity, to make sure we do the right things for the right reasons. Jeremiah warns us that our heart (ego) has the power to deceive even ourselves (Jeremiah 17:9). We become convinced that "this is it" and nothing will move us. When ego reigns, the call has no opportunity. But if we're prepared to submit the process to the test of His ways and Word, then we will be able to discern the difference between chance and call. We must learn to test the opportunity. It could be just chance – just one of those things. It might be that it has come to you because there was no one else, or you just happened to be the best person available at that moment. It could be a God thing, as He opens a door of opportunity for you that you should rush through with all your might. But pause and reflect before you leap.

As I write this chapter, I believe I am in the right place, at the right time, as the right person, with the right gifts doing the right job. Yet, I have to fight with the enemies of my soul on a pretty regular basis – those things that want to entice me out of my God-box and into something that looks good, but isn't the best. This is not an easy struggle and it's one that, in truth, never fully goes away. But it is one in which we can win.

God's box is best. Don't leave it for anything less!

Summary and Reflections

"There are two types of boxes in life, those that restrict us and those that empower us."

What makes us jump boxes?

Crisis

"Crisis truly tests what we believe about the box we're in."

Identify at least 3 things about the box you are in and celebrate them today/this week. *(What happened to you and your context when you focused on celebration?)*

Coveting

"When we covet, we invariably end up choosing for ourselves."

What are the factors about our own lives that cause us to covet someone else's?

Are those conclusions viable?

What happens to your context when you're looking at a "greener field"?

Confidence

"But sometimes when it comes to the God-box we're in, we can face the challenge of both over-confidence and under-confidence."

What are the potential pitfalls when we allow our confidence (over or under) to be the primary driver of any decision we make about our purpose?

Comparison

"Comparison tends to produce certain offspring, namely those of *conformity* and *competition*."

Why is the world so destructive to our mental, emotional and spiritual well being?

Compromise

"Compromise is the 'acceptance of standards that are lower than desirable'."

What circumstances may cause a person to "lower their expectations and standards" in a way that ultimately hurts their purpose?

Chance

"All that glitters isn't gold, and just because we can, doesn't mean we should."

Test every chance:

Does it fit with everything else God has said to me up to this point?
Does it allow me to be the person He made me?
Will it empower me to use the gifts He's given me?
If there was no money on the table, would I still do it?
Is it about ego or purpose?

"God's box is best. Don't leave it for anything less!"

7
OUT OF BOUNDS

What awaits those who jump the boundary and decide to leave their God-designed box? Some will answer, "opportunity, adventure, a bigger world and with it a bigger person...". I love it when people succeed, when they reach new heights and do things they've never done before, things they (or others) never thought was possible. But so often when I witness this, it's not so much that people have "escaped" their box. More often than not, they've simply learned who they are, what they've got and how to use it a whole lot better than before. They've not really left the box, but now they are exploring its outer limits.

Many will reject the very idea of my premise, but the fact that you're still reading this means, for the moment at least, I still have your attention. I reiterate that God's boundaries are not about limitation, but release. He doesn't want to keep us small, He wants us to experience the BIG He's designed – not the big that resides in our ego or some humanistic philosophy. As we've seen, Jesus stayed within God-set boundaries, but was He small?

Paul pursued the "one thing" that God placed before him, but was he small? Limits don't mean limitation. The box God has designed for you will never diminish you. In fact, it's designed to enhance you, because when you look good, so does He!

I've been around long enough to know that some will "listen" to advice but not "hear" what is being said. They will conclude that there's no such thing as a box, and if there is, they should do everything in their power to escape it. So what might await those who venture beyond their God-designed box?

I believe I can fly – ability

Some of the toughest pastoral situations I've dealt with over the years involve a scenario where a person is convinced they are one thing, when everyone else seems to be seeing something else; when they are sure they have a certain gift from God to bless the Church and the world, but everyone in their world (with the exception of their mother) is pretty sure that gift doesn't exist! Often the people in question are sincere, passionate and genuine in what they want to do. Their motivation can be pure and their hearts good, but the problem lies in the fact that they believe they can fly, when clearly they come with no wings attached!

Talent shows both excite and infuriate me. If the point of the show is to seek out genuine talent and give people with real gifts a chance to succeed, that's one thing, but some of our so-called talent shows, driven by the pressure of ratings and the need to make the public laugh, contain elements which distress me. In order for someone to get to stand before a panel of judges on television means that someone, somewhere, deliberately put them through when they clearly did not have the talent they claimed to have. "Set up" by the programme, the nation witnesses a car crash where a sincere (if misled) individual tries to fly without wings. Encouraged perhaps by a family member and fuelled by the dream of being an overnight success, the talent show sets them up for an almighty crash. As we listen to them "singing" we're asking ourselves, "How can someone can get something so obvious so wrong?" But they did and it happens every day.

One of the great dangers of living out of bounds is that we convince ourselves we have the ability to fly when clearly we don't. No one is close enough or strong enough to tell us that we have a "wings issue", and even if they do, well, they're wrong!

I am at the stage in my own journey where I have concluded that if I don't have it then I don't need it. I'm secure enough to let people know I don't have it and no amount of pretending I do have it will make it any better. When we leap the boundary, we have to fake flying and if we're clever we can get away with it for a little while, but sooner or later, someone is going to notice that despite lots of flapping, there ain't no flying!

What can you *actually* do?

Ask yourself that question. Don't ask, "What would I like to do?" or "What would I like to have?" Just answer the simple straightforward question: "What can I *actually* do?'

Why is this question important? It's our ability starting-point. Longing for wings you don't have won't help you fly, but identifying the gifts you do have, the ability and talent that actually resides within you, is an exciting and potentially life-changing starting point. Use what you have where you are right now and see what happens. Too may people live wasteful lives because they have wishful dreams. If God designed you to fly, then wings will be attached somewhere. If you don't have them you don't need them. So rather than lamenting what you don't have, why not identify, celebrate and release what you do have. When you try to live out of bounds, you'll flap but never fly. But within the God-box, you'll touch the stars!

Keeping up appearances – credibility

Pretending is hard work, don't you think? I've never really been good at it and I would have made a rubbish actor, hence the reason I'm not one. I love going to the movies or chilling out in front of the TV with a favourite series. I really do marvel at the ability of actors to take on different personas, kiss others as if they were married to them or as passionate lovers, cry at will and make us believe that what we've just seen is true. But what looks easy on the screen demands enormous energy, hard work, skill, craft, training and discipline. Robert de Niro doesn't just walk onto a set and start acting. Each character requires meticulous preparation so that physically, emotionally, psychologically and professionally, he becomes his character and "puts on" someone else for a few hours each day.

Out of bounds living requires an Oscar performance on an almost daily basis, starting with the person we look at in the mirror. We must first convince ourselves that who we are and where we are is right. All doubts must be squashed. Before we leave the bathroom we need to have our game face on. Only then are we ready to face a world that believes we can fly because we've told them we can. We need to perform every day to maintain the illusion that what they are seeing is flying, when in fact it's not. Exhausted? I am just writing it! The tragedy is that millions live it.

In the Gospels only Jesus used the term hypocrite (maybe because only He could use it). It comes from the word *hupokritḗs* and means essentially "a pretender". But what is interesting is that the word is made up from two other words which, when broken down, mean "under judge". The hypocrite, therefore, is someone who has made a conscious decision to be someone or something that under the surface they are not. This pretence is not accidental or random. It is deliberate, intentional and designed to deceive. This is play-acting of the highest order.

Think about the energy required to pretend. Imagine if you invested the same energy into being the person God has called you to be, and doing the stuff you actually have the ability to do. With only a fraction of the massive energy required to be a hypocrite, you could light up your world with an authentic credibility that rings true everywhere you go.

The opposite of *hypocrisy* is *credibility*. Often film critics will refer to an actor's appearance in a film or play and say they gave a "credible performance". What they really mean is that they were "believeable". They convinced the audience that their character was real and they weren't just playing a role.

To be believable for others, we must first be believable for ourselves. If we can look in the mirror and know that the person looking back isn't a pretence, a mask, a cheap imitation of the real thing, then we'll give our world a chance to meet a real person, who is happy in their own skin and secure in their God-designed box. The problem with pretending is that we have to remember who we were the last time we were there. Credibility on the other hand brings us to liberty. We can rest knowing that what people see is not an "under judge" but the real thing. What they see is who we are! If you're going to live out of bounds then never leave home without a mask. When you stay within your God-box, then your game face is your real face.

When hard work becomes hard work – sustainability

I love what Solomon says:

"All hard work brings a profit, but mere talk leads only to poverty." (Proverbs 14:23)

The Hebrew word translated "hard work" has at its root the idea of pain, toil, even hurt. The type of work being referred to here is costly. It's not talking about a few minutes of hard work, but a long term commitment to doing what is right and good in order to achieve our goal. As I look at this word I see sweat, straining muscles, weary feet and lots of energy.

Even within the God-box, we'll have to engage in hard work. The idea that success will come to us easily is a myth and certainly not a biblical one. As someone once said, "the only place where success comes before work is in the dictionary". How true that is! If we believe that just because we're in our God-box, hard work isn't necessary, then we need to wake up and smell the coffee. Just settle it once and for all: hard work is part of any success story and is always part of God's plan. Check it out if you like, but you won't find God entrusting serious responsibility to a lazy person. If they can't work hard for themselves, why on earth would they work hard for Him?

However, there is hard work and then there's hard work. When we attempt to live out of bounds, I believe hard work moves to another level. It's not just that we are having to work hard, but now everything becomes hard work. There is a toil and cost that we endure happily when we know what we're doing is the right thing and we're the right person to be doing it. Imagine then having to work hard, but knowing that what we're doing isn't really what we should be doing or even where we should be doing it. Suddenly hard work becomes *hard work*!

I love my work. Some have suggested that I'm a workaholic, but genuinely I don't think that is the case. However, I do love what I do. I love going to work, doing my work and being at work. For me pulling a long day or a short day makes no difference, because in spite of the challenges (and there are many), I know it's my box. I know I can live without a mask doing it and I know it's what I'm supposed to be doing. So though it is hard work, though it stretches me, challenges me and sometimes disappoints me, I don't find working hard, hard work.

Recently, I got into a taxi on the way to an airport. I asked the taxi driver how he was and if he had a busy day ahead. We exchanged some pleasantries and then I asked him, "Do you like being a taxi driver?" His reply was instant and insightful: "It's a job!" he said. In those few words I heard the echo of a desperate heart. "What else can I do? It pays the bills. It's better than nothing ... it's a job." I'm sure that young man worked hard that day and did a good job, but by the end of the day, for him as for many others, hard work will have felt like hard work!

Hard work doesn't have to be hard work. When it becomes so, then it is almost impossible to sustain any sense of joy, contentment and excitement regarding our box. We smile, put on a brave face and convince ourselves "it's a job", but deep down we're having to drag every ounce of energy from our souls just to face another day. Out of bounds living makes hard work, hard work. It makes routine costly and energy even more expensive. It makes an eight-hour day feel like a twelve-hour day. It makes what we should be in love with feel like a chore and turns opportunity into an oppressive dread. Sustainability is hard enough when we're living in the God-box, but when we move out of bounds, it becomes a task in itself. We think of getting through a day instead of living in the day. Though we left the God-boundaries for success, survival becomes the aim of the game. When hard work becomes hard work it might be a sign to get back into the God-box.

Filling the gap – availability

When I was younger I loved to play football. As a forty-something plus, I'm still convinced I can play, but my body has warned me on numerous occasions to wise up and enjoy watching it instead. As a teenager, as well as playing for my school, I used to play for East Belfast Liverpool Supporters Club. I got to play in a full Liverpool strip every week (the team I love #YNWA) and our team was pretty good. In fact, as well as having a good run in the league we had reached the semi-final of the cup and were expected to win easily.

All season I had played either up front or in an attacking midfield role, but on the day of the semis, our manager decided to put me at right back! I wasn't even sure where right back was supposed to be. I had never played that position and had no clue what to do. Anyway, I slotted in, but because of my attacking instincts and complete lack of enthusiasm to play at the back, I kept drifting forward (drifting is being kind). I was up the field more than I was back. My manager, with the use of much colourful language, continuously screamed at me to "get back" but I thought I knew better. We lost the semi-final 3-2. An absent right back was partly to blame. I was "released" from my contract and never played for East Belfast Liverpool Supporters Club again! Shame.

We can only be in one place at one time, so if I'm here, I'm not there. As simple as this sounds, we conveniently ignore this truth when it comes to our life position. We know that in the day-to-day, in order to fill one space we must leave another, but what about our God-shaped purpose and our God-designed box? If I make the decision to leave my God-box, although I am filling another space and place, I have left empty the space that God wants me to fill. So who will fill that? The only person who can fill it, of course, is me. But if I'm not there, then it might force someone else to take my place, leaving their place empty and thus putting them in a place where they should not be! Alternatively, my place may simply remain empty, thus impoverishing everyone in my world.

We have to trust the "manager" of our souls to place us in the right places, with the right gifts to do the right things. When we ignore His positioning and convince ourselves that we know best, then we're immediately out of bounds and we will waste time and energy trying to seek out something that fits our talents. Our ambition must be to be available for Him, not simply to pursue our own agenda.

I learned some hard lessons on that semi-final day in Belfast.

Lesson #1: Trust the manager even when you think you know best. To this day I've no idea why my manager put me at right back. With a bit of time and training I may have made a decent right back, but because I didn't like or want it, I mostly abandoned it, probably costing my team a place in the final. Had I trusted him, believed in him and did what he asked, things might have been different – after all, he wanted to win the match too. But I couldn't see that. I thought he was just being stupid or vindictive and so in a battle of wills, I won and we lost.

God knows what He's doing. Furthermore, He's been doing this stuff a long time. He sees the end from the beginning and He has the power to get you to where you need to be. You know what you want, but He knows best. If He's put you there, it's for a reason and it's because He trusts you. So trust Him.

Lesson #2: When you leave your place it may remain empty. Throughout the match, the gaps left by the right back trying to be a centre forward were exploited. Our opposition spotted the weakness and shamelessly capitalised on it. Had I stayed where I was, the back line would have been strong and a couple of their goals may not have happened.

If you and I are not there, we're not there, and therefore all that we should have contributed is lost. We might console ourselves with the fact that someone else could do it, but they can't do it like us. We're all tempted to take on the number 9 centre forward position, even though we're wearing the number 2 right back shirt, but sometimes the most courageous thing to do is to stay put and not move or run.

Lesson #3: Leaving my space may tempt or force others to leave theirs. In order to try and cover the gap I left, other players had to leave their places and in so doing created another gap. The back line became stretched too many times and in an attempt to cover, the cost was high. Good players were stretched too thin and in turn we looked like an average team. Ironically, my selfishness produced selflessness in others, but all in vain in the end. We need to stop thinking that our decisions only affect us and that our lives are only about us, when clearly, everything we are and do impacts somebody somewhere. If I turn up and take my position, I bring energy, life and positivity to my world. But if for whatever reason, I don't turn up, then in turn I create a demotivating context that can hurt those around me. Forcing someone to be selfless by covering for us is quite possibly, one of the most selfish things we can do.

Lesson #4: What I want often ignores what others need. I wasn't thinking of the team, I was thinking only of me. I was angry at the manager and couldn't see why he had put me in that position, so I was going to do what I wanted and that was that. In my selfishness I had lost sight of the honour of playing for and with such a good team, and had made a grave mistake of putting my personal agenda before others.

Mature, successful people understand that the world does revolve around them. They realise they are one part of many and one piece of an incredible jigsaw. They don't storm off when they can't get their own way, and they don't hurt others by demanding their own agenda at the expense of the wider family or team. When we lose sight of the big picture, we're more likely to leave our place and live out of bounds.

Lesson #5: Leaving may cost an opportunity that never comes again. That Saturday was my first and last football semi-final. I've won medals and trophies for running, athletics and judo, but never football, the one game I wanted to win in. We could and should have won that day, but we didn't and the opportunity (for me at least) disappeared forever.

God opportunities are always connected to God positions. When He positions us, when we live in the God-designed box, the right sort of opportunities will always come our way. However, if we leave His box, we may well forfeit His opportunity in pursuit of our own. One cannot be prescriptive about such things, but I am convinced of this: *God cannot give me what He wants to give me if I'm not where He wants me to be*. God's ways are not random, He works to purpose and precision. Though God is generous and gracious, I believe that there are certain opportunities I will only get when I am prepared to stay where He has placed me and live within the boundaries He has set for me.

#Emptyfull? – sanity

#Emptyfull is an expression we've coined in our home and one that I often use on Twitter at the end of a day or season. The idea behind the word is of having given everything – as the Americans might say, "left it all on the park" – and yet feeling very fulfilled at the same time. Though my body may feel depleted, my heart is full. I believe in a place where one can be empty and full at the same time. It sounds like a contradiction and yet I know it to be true.

However, I truly believe that #emptyfull only happens when we are in the right place, being the right person. If we're trying to fly when we can't, or wearing a mask that isn't us, or filling a gap that wasn't meant for us or leaving a place we should be, I think it is almost impossible to live full on the inside. Our physical depletion will only add to our emotional/heart depletion and the latter will cause the former to happen even quicker than normal.

Every day our physical tank gets emptied, whatever box we're in, because we're working hard. But each day our heart also gets emptied as we give ourselves to others, serve, empower, and endeavour to do the best job we can do, at home, work or play. But I have discovered this truth: when I am doing what I ought to be doing, in the way I ought to be doing it, my heart tank is replenished by the purpose itself and the sense of connectedness and completeness it gives. This doesn't mean that we should ignore our hearts. I work hard at doing the sorts of things that assist inner replenishment. But, in truth, we don't have to try too hard to do it when we are in the God-box for our lives.

If at the end of every day or week we are empty on the inside, something is not quite right. If what we're doing is draining us of all life and joy, we at least need to step back and ask why? The God-box will demand hard work of us, as we've already seen, but doing what He wants, using the gifts He's given us, will naturally and supernaturally fill us from the inside out. Out of bounds living is truly tempting, especially if we are not where we want to be. But before you jump the fence, beware and be wise.

Summary and Reflections

"God's boundaries are not about limitation, but release."

I believe I can fly – ability

"It's our ability starting-point. Longing for wings you don't have won't help you fly, but identifying the gifts you do have, the ability and talent that resides within you, is an exciting and potentially life-changing starting point."

*What can you **actually** do? (Not just what you'd like to do)*

*What gifts have you **actually** got? (Not just what you'd like to have)*

Keeping up appearances – credibility

"Out of bounds living requires an Oscar performance on an almost daily basis..."

If you have to pretend to be someone else to do what you are currently doing, should you be doing it? God's box will always celebrate you!

When working hard becomes hard work – sustainability

"Working hard doesn't have to be hard work. When it becomes so, then it is almost impossible to sustain any sense of joy, contentment and excitement regarding our box."

When you do what you do, are you exhausted or excited?

Filling the gap – availability

"I can only be in one place at one time, so if I'm here, I'm not there."

Look afresh at your life. In what areas are you making a unique and necessary contribution? What would happen if you didn't "turn up" today; if you refused to be available?

#Emptyfull – sanity

"...when I am doing what I ought to be doing, in the way I ought to be doing it, my heart tank is replenished by the purpose itself and the sense of connectedness and completeness it gives."

Is your current job, ministry context or activity filling your tank as you do it? When you are doing what you're doing, is your heart replenished or impoverished?

8
ENJOY HIS JOURNEY — FUN

I remember seeing a programme on the life and times of David Attenborough, perhaps one of the most well travelled men on the planet. I was fascinated to see all the places he had been to, the animals he had encountered and the adventures he'd had. Yet I was amazed to discover that when he travels, he packs a medium size suitcase. In fact, he's had the same medium size suitcase for many years. I was sure he'd have trunks of stuff with all sorts in them, but no, experience had taught this man to take only what he needed for a particular journey – and that's exactly what he does.

However, I would suggest to you that David Attenborough is exceptional (in more ways than one) in this area. Most, if not all of us, suffer from the temptation to pack too much stuff when going on a journey. We know what we need, but for some the definition of "need" encompasses things that would be deemed unnecessary by others. It's amazing isn't it, you can have two people going on the same journey and one has two bags and the other has five bags. Yet the person with five bags can and will justify everything they have in them, convinced their bags are "necessary" for the journey.

The Psalmist says,

"Blessed are those whose strength is in you, who have set their hearts on pilgrimage." (Psalm 84:5)

The word translated pilgrimage הָלִּסְמ (*mesillah*) points to the idea of a highway; of a way cast up, like an embankment. In other words, a definable and distinguishable way – something that is deliberate, not accidental. The pilgrimage is not something we're stumbling into, but a pathway we've deliberately taken. In fact, the nuance is even stronger that the pathway/highway being spoken of here is not just a physical one, but one that is in the heart. The pilgrim walks a physical path because they have a spiritual path. The outer journey is being driven by inner conviction and vision. The Hebrew phrase literally reads, "in whose heart the ways in (are)".

I love how the English Standard Version puts it:

"Blessed are those whose strength is in You, in whose heart are the highways to Zion."

We're all on a journey, but God wants it to be a journey of the heart! It is so easy to be caught up with deadlines, hopes, dreams, expectations, pressure, failures and successes! That's a lot for anybody to cope with. Life is a serious business and many people have become so serious about it that they have forgotten how to enjoy it.

Some time ago, friends of mine bought me a book entitled *Eeyore's Little Book of Gloom*. The back cover reads, "A leaden collection of Pessimistic Ponderings from the 100 Acre Wood's resident cynic. Perfect for those who are tired of Life or tedious little tomes full of Joy." For those of you who know the Winnie the Pooh stories written by A.A. Milne, you will know that Eeyore is dominated by a negative outlook on life, and usually his feelings rule his reactions. His droopy ears, sad eyes and pinned-on tail all add to the blueness of his existence – that and the fact that he is after all a blue donkey!

Some of the things Eeyore comes out with are positively depressing (did I just do an oxymoron?) and if these are an expression of what he truly believes, it's no wonder this donkey is struggling.

Let me give you a sample:

Invisible Mending
You can give a donkey a happy ending ... but the miserable beginning remains forever.

Gaze on Greyness
Cultivate a permanently tragic expression by staring at your reflection for hours on end; it's sure to bring a touch of gloom to even the sunniest of days.

Expect the worst
Even if someone remembers to come to your birthday party, they will almost certainly eat your present on the way ... or break it!

And finally, "Things can only get wetter"![1] Of course, life is serious and we shouldn't ignore that reality, but Eeyore saw the serious side of life because it was "in his heart".

The pathway within us will determine in many ways our

capacity for joy, hope and fun on the journey.

Look at the example of Jesus. *Was there anyone who had a life purpose more serious than His?*

Of course not. Yet, He danced at weddings, played with children, had real friendships and attracted people with His zest for life. Yes, life is a serious business, but we can do it much better with some joy in our hearts.

God's preoccupation is not just our destination, but also the quality of our journey. He wants us to make it to the end, but I believe He would like us to enjoy getting there. We must understand that the destination is important, but not at the expense of the journey, for the Bible teaches we cannot have one without the other. If we learn to journey well, we will engage with destiny on the way to our destination; we will enjoy the experience of living and growing in God, and we will achieve that which God has purposed for us to do. The greatest key to journeying well and enjoying the journey in the process is learning to stay within the God-box for our lives. If we stay within His boundaries, not only will we go further than we thought, but we'll have some fun on the way.

Are we there yet?

As a parent of three children, I have had the experience that millions of others have shared. Bags packed, car loaded up, kids in the back, and half an hour into a 6-hour journey a voice comes from behind: "Are we there yet?" My response to this oft-repeated question normally starts out Christ-like and descends rapidly from there.

"We've only just left pet, we'll be there soon."

Are we there yet?

"No not yet, just read your book."

Are we there yet?

"Put your headphones on and watch the dvd!"

Are we there yet?

"No we're not. When we are you'll be the first to know!"

Are we there yet?

"Ask me that stupid question once more and the first thing we'll be performing when we arrive will be your funeral!"

Get the picture?

Kids of a certain age have no concept of time or journey. If we tell them we're going to Ireland for our holidays, they've no idea of the scale of the journey. They just want to arrive and get on with the holiday. I'm an adult and I like arriving, but I've had to learn that the journey is part of the holiday and that making the most of that journey is as important as reaching the destination.

It's hard to enjoy the journey when all we're thinking about is arriving. I've learned this, not only on my journeys but in life. Too often we're looking at the purpose of our lives as something we'll arrive at eventually, when a more biblical understanding of purpose is that it's something we live in constantly.

My wife will tell you that I'm a bit of a control freak when it comes to journeys. If we're supposed to be at the airport an hour before, I like to add on another 30 minutes. I like sitting in the lounge, chilling, have a second coffee and getting ready for the flight. I hate the idea of pushing, pulling and running through airports like a maniac, because our gate is about to close. These situations make great stories over dinner, but they're terrible to live through at the time. I've found that the more I plan, the more I enjoy and so by the time I get there, I'm usually in decent shape emotionally. I think my youngest daughter, Beth-Anne, is catching onto this. When we were planning our holiday this year, it involved a boat sailing of about 2 hours. I had upgraded us to premier so we could get priority boarding and exit, as well as access to a great lounge on board. As I was booking, Beth-Anne spotted that for an extra £20 we would have our very own bedroom suite, with double bed, TV and shower. "Let's do it Dad, book it now!" I tried to explain we'd only be on the boat for 2 hours at most. "But Dad, it's a bed!" Seems she's keen to enjoy the journey as well!

Here is there!

I know you're keen to get there, but here is there! I know what people mean when they talk about "arriving at God's purpose" for their lives, but that creates the impression that purpose has an arrival point, when really purpose is a journey – His journey. What did David say?

"...in whose heart are the highways to Zion."

The sooner we understand that here is there, the faster we'll start enjoying His journey. We'll stop fighting with now and start embracing the opportunities before us. We'll stop despising now and start celebrating what is around us. We'll stop complaining about now and start living in the possibilities of what is within us!

Too many miss "here" because they're always looking for "there". When we live like this, it is almost impossible to have fun on the way and it becomes more and more difficult for joy, hope and rest to stay with us on the journey. Remember, process doesn't take us to purpose; process is part of the purpose. The road we're on isn't leading us to our destination, it forms part of our destination. If we can find a way to enjoy this moment, then the chances are here will become part of there, and when that happens, we'll enjoy His journey and ours much more!

Did you pack the contents of your case sir?

I always have a little moral dilemma every time I'm asked that question at an airport. Technically the answer is no, because Dawn my wife always packs my case before a trip. But I was there in the room when she did it. However, apart from laying clothes and travel items on the bed (not all of which make it past my packer-upper wife), I didn't have any part in actually packing the case. So how do I answer? "Of course I did!" (Liar! Sinner! "Please forgive me Lord and don't let the plane crash because of my sin!")

Seriously, if the packing was left to me, I'd need a greater weight allowance on every trip and I still wouldn't get everything in. I'm a very tidy and neat person, but when it comes to packing, I lose all ability to reason and coordinate. It's always a worry when I'm flying home and Dawn's not there to pack! I usually end up asking myself the question, "How on earth did she get all that in there? That's impossible. It's a miracle!"

So how do you pack for the journey?

Do you recognise yourself in the following examples?

The Complacent packer

This is the "last minute" packer – the person who breezes through life and just nonchalantly throws things into a bag the night before. They don't think about the journey too much. Neither do they care about the impact their lack of preparation and investment might have on others, because they believe that someone, somewhere will bail them out.

I love my son, but he's just a touch (okay a lot) like this. In

2013 he went off with a friend to Kenya for nine weeks to work on a fabulous Christian project. He left most of his packing to the night before, choosing to celebrate with his friends from the church, rather than be at home packing and getting to bed early (young people!).

On the morning we left I asked him if he had everything, passport, money, bag, camera, clean underpants, you know the drill. He said yes and we climbed into the car and headed for Heathrow. As we were just about to get onto the motorway, he shouted, "I've forgot my camera!" So because we had time (because I'm a control freak and we left early), we were able to go back and get his camera. One final check: "Have you got everything?" After being assured he had, we headed off. When we got to the airport we discovered he had left most of his cash behind (which we had to wire to Kenya later), and when we got home we then found out that he had left his malaria tablets on the table beside his bed! I love my son, but ... you fill in the blanks!

In truth he got away with it because of the people around him, but had he been on his own, the outcomes would have been much more impacting and even dangerous. When we take this sort of nonchalant attitude to the journey, we inevitably miss stuff and create burdens that others have to carry. We make other people's journeys more challenging because we're not taking our own seriously!

The Contingency packer

As I've said, when I go on any trip, unless it's an overnight stay somewhere, Dawn packs my bags. There are two main reasons why she does this.

Firstly, she's brilliant at it. She can get stuff in a suitcase that I just didn't think was possible and, furthermore, it comes out looking good and not like a dog's dinner.

Secondly, she vets what I want to put in. Invariably she'll ask the questions, "Why do you want that? ... What's this for? ... Are you sure you need three suits considering you're only preaching once? ... How many pairs of shoes does any one man need? ... Put the dog down!" etc.

This process forces me to ask myself, "Do I really need this for the journey?" The temptation I face is to pack for things I think *might* happen, even though nothing is planned. I play it safe and pack all manner of things under the "just in case" banner. I must confess to you (but don't tell anyone, especially Dawn) that I have subsequently sneaked stuff into my case when she wasn't looking!

The temptation is to take everything we think we might need for every eventuality, when we need to have the confidence to take only what we do need. I'll touch on this more later in the chapter, but this is a massive key to enjoying His journey. If we keep trying to carry what we don't need, it's only going to weigh us down for the journey He wants us to make. If we're prepared to travel light, but with all we need, we can make the journey without experiencing a spiritual hernia!

The Comfort packer

This is the person who will pack stuff that just makes them feel better about the trip. They'll include the things they really like, their favourite stuff, even though for this trip, it isn't needed at all. "Having all my stuff just makes me feel better," they say. I understand that, but the more journeys you make, the more the "feel better" stuff accumulates. Before you know it, the stuff designed to make you feel better starts to take a counter-productive toll on your journey.

Growing up means moving beyond the "feel good" stuff and into a "this is the right thing to do" mentality. Comfort and feeling good is something we all desire and want, but even when we're making His journey, the right journey, it isn't always possible to have everything we want, or would like. I have had the joy of travelling to some truly stunning places and I've been through quite a few passports, but I have rarely if ever been on a trip that has been absolutely perfect, or where I got everything I wanted or we managed to do everything as we hoped or imagined. If feeling good is too important to me, then no element of the journey will feel worthwhile, because even on the best of days, there's always something that conspires to rain on our parade!

The Control packer

This is the person who wants to feel that no matter what comes their way, they are in control; that they have what they need for every situation so that they will always be in control and nothing will go wrong. So the medical kit grows from a strip of plasters and a few paracetamol to something resembling the mobile unit of our local hospital. There's a strong possibility they're going to be stopped for drug running!

The control packer takes books they will never read, a supersize shampoo for an overnight stay and a needle and thread, just in case, even though they can't sew!

The control freak lives to some extent within us all, but trying to control the journey is the fastest way of driving the joy and fun from it. There is nothing wrong with planning and good preparation, but when we move from that to trying to orchestrate every element of every situation in every moment, a crash and burn episode is about to happen! Few people like to be told to chill, but there are moments when that is exactly what we have to do. Some situations on the journey are just out of our control – and even if they weren't, there are times when the right thing to do is let things be, not try to control them.

Travel tips for enjoying His journey

Pack for Purpose

I remember watching a program about Bedouins in North Africa. It was incredible to see a family pack up their home and be ready to move in under an hour and a half. The reason they were able to pack up so quickly was because their focus was the journey and their purpose, not their stuff. All that they had was subservient to their purpose. They couldn't have stuff they could not pack up quickly and move easily. They learned to live and travel light.

There is a lesson here for us. To truly enjoy the journey we must understand the purpose of the journey and order our lives accordingly. That will stop us from living for the wrong thing, accumulating the wrong stuff and trying to pack it all into our suitcase. If we know we're going to a sundrenched beach, then thermal underwear is not required. If our journey is going to take us to a frozen wasteland, leave the bikini at home! I know these are silly examples, but so often when it comes to our spiritual journey, we jettison all common sense, and sometimes with it simple rules and processes that will help us journey well.

Do you want to enjoy His journey? Then be clear on the

purpose and pack accordingly.

Take only what you need

If we are not careful, the focus of our journey is hijacked by stuff we're carrying with us and we lose sight of the reason we're making the journey in the first place. Whatever we carry with us should be there to serve the purpose of the journey. When the things we take become more important than the journey itself, then we are in big trouble.

In a slightly different context, but with a similar picture in mind, the Message puts brilliantly what the writer to the Hebrews says:

"Strip down and start running – and never quit! No extra spiritual fat, no parasitic sins. Keep your eyes on Jesus, who both began and finished this race we're in." (Hebrews 12:1-2)

Many don't enjoy the journey of life because they're carrying too much stuff. They believe they can make it with an overweight bag, which is getting heavier by the minute! They have lost sight of why they got on the journey in the first place. Their lives have become so cluttered with things, with issues, with hang-ups, with sin, with those things deemed vital, that they can't remember the last time they actually sat back and just enjoyed life and sucked in the journey they are on.

We all know there can be a cost for carrying excess baggage. An airline will give you a fairly generous weight allowance, but if you exceed it, they will likely charge you for the privilege, because your excess is starting to affect everyone else. How many times have I seen someone transfer weight from a bag into either their hand luggage, or even onto their person. I have witnessed people wearing multiple layers of clothing to escape the charge. The irony is, however, that wherever they try to shift the weight, they're still carrying it, one way or the other. Some people are good at "shifting the weight", moving it from one place to another and making everyone around them think that everything is okay, but 40kgs is 40kgs no matter how you cut it, and someone has to carry it!

When Jesus was sending out His young disciples, He undoubtedly shocked them with His directives:

"Do not take along any gold or silver or copper in your belts; take no bag for the journey, or extra tunic, or sandals or a staff; for the worker is worth his keep." (Matthew 10:9-10).

Jesus wanted His followers to travel as light as possible for their particular journey (I don't think He expected this to be the pattern for every journey, but it should remain the principle). He was removing from them the normal human temptation to take more than they needed, to pack for every contingency, taking their favourite coat and ensuring they had enough money for every eventuality. Jesus stripped all that away from them for one reason: He wanted them to focus on why they were on the journey not on the stuff for the journey. Excess baggage was not an issue for this journey. He ensured that only the purpose dominated.

Why should someone else carry what you can't?

I have a travel rule when I'm running short term mission trips around the world: "If you can't carry your bag, no one else will." Now, I know some well meaning Christian is going to have a go at me for discouraging my teams from loving one another and "carrying each others burdens". Such a person has clearly never lead 12-15 people around the world on a testing trip, involving various modes of transport including planes, vans, cars, buses and trains. Yes, we are called to carry each other's burdens, but Jesus didn't say anything about over-packed, over-weight bags on a missions trip! Of course (let me be slightly more Christian here), I'm not talking about those with illness or those who through disability can't carry a case. I'm talking about those who pack too much stuff, can't move it off their bed and expect someone else to do the heavy lifting.

Here's the thing to remember: "It's your bag!" One of the great principles of life is take care of your own bag. You pack it (unless you're me, in which case Dawn packs it), you carry it, you check it and you pick it up off the carrier belt. It is not the responsibility of anyone else to sort your bag – it's yours! The sooner we realise this and do something about it, the happier we'll be. The sooner we stop expecting others to carry what we've packed, the quicker we'll come to terms with the stuff we're putting in our "bag". If we have to carry it, we'll be much more careful about what we put in it!

Remember also, if someone has to carry your bag, that will impact and effect their journey. They may be big and strong, but their journey will get tougher if they have to carry yours and theirs. Again, don't mishear me, we are all called to bear each other's burdens, but we aren't talking about burdens here, we're talking about stuff you're trying to cram into your life-bag that you don't need and expect other people to manage. If we're packing for purpose and taking only what we need then we should be able to carry our own bag. If we can't carry it, it may be because we've got stuff in there we don't need!

What's in your bag?

Do you really need it?

Is it helping you or getting in the way?
Are you spending more energy on what's in the case, instead of the journey itself?

One of the keys to enjoying His journey is learning to travel light. We have to learn to take only what we need for the journey of purpose, ruthlessly jettisoning the stuff that isn't important, necessary or useful.

Look at Jesus. Was there anyone happier, more focused on their journey? Yet look at how light He travelled. What He didn't need, He didn't take, allowing Him to fulfil His purpose and enjoy His journey. He stayed within His God-box and had the courage to only put the stuff He needed into His bag. Maybe that's why He danced so well at weddings, because nothing was weighing Him down!

His Journey awaits you. Have fun on the way and enjoy it!

Summary and Reflections

Fun

"...they walk a physical path because they have a spiritual path... the outer journey is being driven by an inner conviction and vision!"

"It's hard to enjoy the journey when all we're thinking about is arriving."

Travel tips for enjoying the journey

Pack for purpose

"All they had was subservient to the purpose."

Take only what you need

"Strip down and start running..."

Why should someone else carry what you can't?

"The sooner we stop expecting others to carry what we've packed, the quicker we'll come to terms with the stuff we're putting in our bag."

If you were only packing for purpose...

What do you actually "need" to take with you?

What luxuries are in your bag? i.e. the things you want but don't actually need!

Are there things in your bag that you're expecting others to carry for you?

Footnotes:

1. Eeyore's Little Book of Gloom, 1999, inspired by A.A.Milne and E.H.Shepard.

9
REALISED POTENTIAL — FRUITFULNESS

Potential is a double-edge word. By very definition it represents what could be, what something or someone might be capable of being or becoming, and it expresses possibility. It's a word that carries the "potential" of hope, fulfilment, success and realisation. But the brightness of potential also highlights its dark side, in that what could be, might not be; what something or someone might be capable of being or becoming, might not happen and the possibility might never get to be realised! We tend to think of potential in others and ourselves as positively as possible (and rightly so), but I've been around long enough to know that not every opportunity is taken and not every beginning gets the ending it deserves.

A vast army of people stood before a river with an unshakeable promise, the resource and the means to cross over, and literally a land of opportunity before them, but they chose to climb out of the God-box and do what they thought was best. As a result, a whole generation of people never realised their potential and instead of feasting on milk and honey, they learned to be creative with manna (Numbers 13-14).

A king recruited a young musician to his service. But soon the psalmist demonstrated his potential in leadership and war. The young man had the potential to not only serve the king, but make him look better than he ever dreamed. But what God gave as opportunity, Saul took as a threat, and in a moment of madness tried to nail David's potential to the wall. The day David fled, Saul lost more than a servant; he lost his future (1 Samuel 16-19).

Potential is a magnificent word, but be careful not to use it in the wrong way, which I fear too many fall into the trap of doing.

Potential becomes an excuse

Over the years I've seen too many people hide behind the excuse of potential, excusing either themselves or others. Someone comes up short and we say "They've got potential". As we'll see later in the chapter, we all need good coaches who see what we can be and believe we can make it. But if we keep coming up short, if we keep failing, if we keep missing the mark, then it's probably about something other than potential. To simply assign these moments or this pattern to potential is to do a disservice to the person in question and the truth of what potential actually is. Everyone has potential, of that I am convinced, but we can make it the excuse for every shortcoming or missed opportunity. Staying within the God-box gives us a better chance of seeing our potential become a reality.

Potential becomes an escape

"One day it will work out. One day I'll make it. One day, some day, possibility will become reality." Again, I believe this, and even as I write, I am intentionally working towards the God-given potential that still resides within me. But we must not live in the escapism of tomorrow while missing the opportunity and possibility of today. One day or some day must not eclipse today! If we are not careful we live in Neverland, a sort of parallel universe, which permits us to swap the reality of now for the fantasy of tomorrow. I've discovered a relentless and unshakeable principle in life: in order to get to tomorrow, I must go through today. Today may not be what we want. We may not be where we want to be. But it is what it is, and it's on those days that our gifts, talents and potential must come to the fore. Don't allow escapism to pervert the purity of the potential that lies within you. If you escape from today, tomorrow will escape from you!

Potential becomes an existence

I don't want "he had potential" on my gravestone! Whenever I go, I want to have lived before I died and hopefully not only appreciated my potential, but realised it. God wants us to live a fruitful and productive life. He does not want us trapped in the dead-zone of "might have been", "could have been" or "should have been". Rather, He longs for us to discover the life-giving world of God-box living and the joy of producing fruitful lives. When it comes to potential our mentality should be that of a pilgrim not a settler. We're making a journey through, but we're not planning to hang around. Don't settle for the land of potential when the world of purpose awaits.

We define potential as the "possible as opposed to actual; capable of being or becoming and expressing possibility".

I believe that by staying within our God-designed boundaries, we have a better chance of experiencing the realisation of our potential. God created what lies within you and it's His ambition to bring it out, so your world can see how awesome He is and how amazing you are.

There are four key truths to remember as we seek to realise our God-given potential:

Success is in the seed

As I write this chapter, much of the world is gripped with World Cup fever, which is being held in Brazil. Twenty-two year old Brazilian footballer Neymar is not only the face of the 2014 World Cup, but the hopes of his nation rest on him to inspire his team and bring the coveted trophy home to Brazil for the sixth time. I suppose if they win he'll be a "god", and if they don't, he'll need to emigrate. I hear Northern Ireland have a vacancy for the number 10 shirt!

Though Neymar's face seems to occupy every billboard in Brazil, few will have heard of or recognise his first coach, Betinho Santos, the man who first spotted Neymar's amazing talent. His parents were so poor they couldn't even afford to take their son to his first club for training, so his coach stepped in. He said,

"Wherever you need to go I'll drive you."

Explaining why he did this, he said of the young Neymar, "He was a diamond that needed to be cut; a little diamond, a rough one, just waiting for someone to polish it, and pretty soon he will become the best player in the whole world."[1]

It seems he was right. Betinho identified what was already there and did everything in his power to nurture the "little diamond".

However, what Neymar has become he already was, his success was in the seed.

To the uneducated and uninterested, one seed may look roughly the same as another, but if we could look within the seed, we'd see everything that will turn that seed into an orange tree or a rose bush. Everything needed to "become" is already within the seed, and given the chance, all the potential within that seed will grow into all it was designed to be.

To most people in Praia Grande, his home town, little Neymar looked just like all the other boys kicking a ball in the street, but Betinho saw the seed of something great and now the world is starting to see what he saw all those years ago.

The seed cannot become something other than what lies within. So it is with you. The seeds of your success already lie within you, put there by God at the moment of your conception. Everything you were meant to become is seeded within you. When we try to become someone or something other than what's seeded within, we set ourselves up for pain and disappointment and a life of unrealised potential.

Jesus borrowed the boat of a young fisherman as a platform to teach the gathered crowd. After His teaching session was over, Jesus invited the young man to put his boat out into the deep to catch some fish. Though young Simon was somewhat skeptical, he obeyed and they caught so many fish that they needed another boat to help haul in the catch! At the end of the story, Jesus said to Simon,

"Don't be afraid; from now on you will catch men." (Luke 5:10)

Simon (Peter) may have thought he was seeded to catch fish for a living, but little did he know he was seeded to catch men for God. He could have made a decision to reject God's box, but fortunately he had the wisdom to grasp the opportunity and live a life of realised potential in God's purpose, rather than a life of quiet desperation by the lake (Luke 5:1-11).

We are only capable of being what is within our being. Some settle for less and many try to be more, but both are natural expressions of a broken and fallen world. Few, it seems, have the courage of contentment – to recognise what they are and live within the glorious freedom of those boundaries. If we stick to the design within the seed, success is inevitable, whatever it looks like!

Coached to cause

In the summer of 2012, London hosted the Olympic Games and Team GB exceeded our wildest dreams. In a summer of success, we landed 29 gold, 17 silver and 19 bronze medals. One of our medalists was 19 year old Jade Jones who won Britain's first ever Olympic gold in taekwondo. I remember her achievement more than others because of her joy on winning. Her smile and laughter were mesmerising and her uncontainable zest saw her dance around the arena.

She beat Yuzhuo Hou 6-4 to take the women's -57kg title and avenge the Chinese fighter's sudden-death win at the 2011 World Championships. After a nervous opening with few scoring opportunities, Jones took control of the final in the second round and powered to victory. On winning the gold she said this:

"My coach is a legend and without him I wouldn't have been anywhere near where I was today. When I came out, I just wanted to go on and win."[2]

In a moment of personal glory when the whole world was watching, she remembered her coach.

Paul and Barnabas were great friends who pioneered new ground together in the first recorded missionary journey to the Gentile world. They had been through thick and thin together, but in Acts 15 they decided to go their separate ways over a young man called John Mark. He had left (deserted) the two warriors on their first journey and now on the eve of their second trip, Barnabas wanted to give him a second chance and take him, but Paul was having none of it. The men agreed to disagree and went off in different directions, but the text says this:

"Barnabas took Mark and sailed for Cyprus." (verse 39)

Years later, in some of the last recorded words of Paul, he wrote these words:

"Get Mark and bring him with you, because he is helpful to me in my ministry." (2 Timothy 4:11)

Mark was not only useful to Paul, but to the worldwide Church, as the first man to record the life of Jesus in his gospel!

It seems the work of Barnabas the coach paid off.

When Paul went off on his second trip with Silas, but without Barnabas and Mark, he arrived at Lystra and while there met a young disciple called Timothy. The text reveals his potential:

"The brothers at Lystra and Iconium spoke well of him." (Acts 16:2)

Paul took the young man and coached him. He would later become a great leader and a foremost influencer in the church at Ephesus, one of the greatest churches in the New Testament. From a prison cell Paul wrote these words:

"I hope in the Lord Jesus to send Timothy to you soon ... I have no one else like him, who takes a genuine interest in your welfare ... But you know that Timothy has proved himself, because as a son with his father he has served with me in the work of the gospel."(Philippians 2:19-22)

It seems the work of Paul the coach paid off.

Barnabas saw the potential in Mark and Paul saw the potential in Timothy. Both men invested, sacrificed and empowered these young men and, as a result, they realised something of their potential in God and richly impacted their worlds. Both Mark and Timothy benefitted from the coaching of these great pioneers and I am sure that everyone involved was enlarged, including the coaches.

Great coaches see the seed; they see what someone can become, because they understand what they are. Great coaches persist, they invest and they relentlessly pursue greatness in the other. They so want those in their care to succeed, that it hurts them deeply when they don't.

My father passed into the presence of Jesus on 9th December 2013. He didn't leave us much in the way of material wealth, but he did deposit a legacy of love that continues to empower me today. He became a Christian at 10 and loved Jesus all his life. He would have loved to have gone to Bible College, but never got the chance, but he served Jesus and His Church all his life. When I was around 10-11 years old, he took me down to the famous shipbuilders, Harland and Wolfe, where he had worked for many years. He took me to the "moulding shop" and explained his routine. Then he took me to see some of the furnaces, where for a few extra pounds per week, he would clean them out. As we stood in this massive, adult world, I was overwhelmed by the smells, sight, sounds and scale of my daddy's world. This is where he came to every day! As we stood under the great furnace we looked up and he said something to me I shall never forget: "John, I am working down here so you don't have to!"

In truth, I didn't really get it then, but later I did. My dad was laying down himself to invest and empower his children. He served his world so that I could discover mine. There is hardly a day goes by when I don't think about my dad and his words.

It seems the work of my dad the coach paid off!

If you're coaching a Mark, Timothy or even a John, *don't give up*. You may be the means of getting their little diamond to their world!

Fruit comes out of root

In his book *Visioneering*, Andy Stanley concluded, "There is a tendency to confuse success with the rewards of success." He added, "If you are where God wants you, fulfilling the responsibilities He has given you, you are successful. In fact, when that is the case, you are as successful as you will ever be."[3]

We do tend to get caught up with what we believe success looks like. In the world of the internet we have more access to more stuff than ever, and from a living room or coffee shop we can see what other people's world of success looks like. The danger is that we want what success looks like for *them*, instead of understanding what it might look like for *us*! If our desire for success is being shaped by the experience of another, then we risk never being satisfied with our own achievements and the disappointment of having less than someone else.

Basing your evaluation of success on someone else's box is rootless living, which ultimately will produce anything but fruit. If we want to produce fruit that enriches others and truly expresses who we are, then it must come out of authentic rootedness in who we believe we are and what we are called to do.

The root from which fruit comes has within it two dynamic

elements. The first is *Truth*. There are many elements to this and as truth reaches deep, it has many branches drilling into the soil. However, I have discovered and held to four aspects of *root truth*.

The Truth of who God is

Our view of God is vital to our success. A distorted view of Him leaves us truly rootless and subject to any whim of philosophy or thinking that comes our way. As we've seen previously in this book, it is a confession about who God is that lies at the heart of both the Old and New Testament communities. When we know who He is, we can stand.

The Truth of what God has said

The first recorded words of God the Father to Jesus in the Gospels are a powerful affirmation of His commitment to His Son. This I believe becomes the bedrock on which Jesus builds His ministry for the next three years. When under pressure, when facing relentless temptation, when misunderstood and unappreciated, I believe Jesus recalled the words of His Father that day:

"You are My Son, whom I love; with You I am well pleased." (Luke 3:22)

On a weekly basis I go back to the promises God the Father has made to me, the words He has given me, and I remind both my Father and myself of the power of these words. When I'm tempted to leave the box, do my own thing, adjust the timeline and create my own world, I go back to the simplicity of His promises and the unswerving nature of His Word. If He said it He will do it and that settles it!

The Truth of who I am

This has been the single biggest revelation that has transformed my life and thinking. I have had to wrestle with what my own mind tries to invent about me, what the world around me may think of me, and even what the enemy of my soul wants to tell me. I have to keep coming back to *who I am in Christ*. I have come to accept and believe that I am a child of God's grace and that I am His masterpiece, created by Him and for Him. There are days when my feelings try to boss these truths, but I'm pleased to say, most days, the truth wins!

The Truth of my call

Being a follower of Jesus is amazing enough, but to have the privilege of serving the Living God is mind-blowing for me. There are days when I wake up and wonder how I got here. I remember the moment my life changed as a fifteen year old, supposedly revising for my O-levels one Sunday evening while everyone was at church. In truth my heart was growing cold towards the Lord and I was trying to find my own way without Him. But I remember the living room filling with His presence. I stopped what I was doing and lay face down on the floor. I sensed (maybe I heard God's voice) that the Lord was offering me a choice. That night, in a little room in Belfast, Yahweh filled the space and offered a backslidden boy a God-shaped box and a God-designed future. That night, I surrendered and I have never unsurrendered!

In reality, these four simple but powerful truths have formed the root system of truth from which my life grows. These truths have held me and protected me from my own stupidity and arrogance. These truths have strengthened me when the success of others was "greater" than mine. These truths have produced in me and through me eternal fruit.

The second root of the fruit is *Trust*.

To trust Father God when everything within us wants to take control is a constant challenge to any human being. Desire for success, short cuts to success and the need for success will provoke us to stop trusting and start trying to do life in our own strength.

Trust says – even if people don't know, God knows

Most within the Church would scorn the cult of celebrity and fame, but if we're honest, we're all susceptible to it. Someone unfollows us on Facebook or Twitter and we want to know why. No one notices our act of kindness and we get a little annoyed. Others seem to get the glory for our hard work – well that's just not fair! See what I mean? Most of us don't want to be famous, but we do want to be noticed and nothing gets us noticed like success. But we must be careful to protect our hearts against the allure of applause rather than purpose. It's nice when people notice, but even when they don't, we've still done the right thing and eventually, if not immediately, that will get its reward. Trust stops worrying whether people notice, because it knows God does!

Trust says – His rewards are enough

I love what Paul says to the church at Galatia:

"Let us not become weary in doing good, for at the proper time we will reap a harvest if we do not give up." (Galatians 6:9)

Note that Paul recognises that doing the right thing can be

wearying, especially if there's no immediate or noticeable reward. He draws our attention to the "proper time" and urges us not to give up, because trusting God in doing good can sometimes be a challenge, especially when we don't seem to be getting what our actions deserve or the harvest for the seeds we put into the ground. *Trust* coupled with *truth*, empowers us to hold on for His rewards, regardless of what may or may not be coming our way. Rewards sometimes come immediately, but sometimes they take weeks, months or even years. Trust isn't discouraged by this. Trust knows that His rewards are enough and they'll come, eventually!

Trust says – the right thing done the right way will produce the right fruit

Remember Galatians 6:9? Verse 10 carries on to say,

"Therefore, as we have opportunity, let us do good to all people, especially to those who belong to the family of believers."

Note the phrase, "as we have opportunity". We don't have to wait for a call, a special moment or an invitation, we can simply, in our everyday context learn to do the good that flows out of our God-box. Trust comes back to the truth that good is good, no matter what. Wherever and however, good is always good and good will, at some point, get the harvest it deserves.

A leader was once asked the question, "What's the secret of success?" He answered, "Doing the right thing, long enough!" Trust keeps doing the right thing, in the right way, because trust knows good will ultimately produce an incredible harvest.

When truth and trust form our root system, the outcome is fruit – God fruit – fruit that will not only last, but fruit that is an authentic expression of who we are and the God-box we live within!

Some things are possible

Potential, by its very definition, points to the fact that not everything is possible. Realised potential is not the random outcome of unconnected events, but rather the outworking of what is already within us. Those who understand this and become content within their God-box are intentional about what they have and how that may be used for the glory of God. It is no coincidence then that people with this mentality will be among the most successful we know. They understand that not everything is possible, but that some things are. Ironically, it's when we achieve some things that people in their excitement start saying, "anything is possible!"

Accepting "some things" is not defeatist – it's genius. It liberates us from the tyranny of "everything" and empowers us to live joyfully in the freedom of some things. Many will never realise their potential because what they are trying to realise isn't there. They are trying to become someone they are not and trying to do something they haven't got the tools for. The happiest people I know and the most successful people I've encountered are those who live in the freedom of some things. However, because they focus and live with such intention, it looks like they are doing more than they actually are, when in reality, they are just doing some things exceptionally well!

We were all created with the potential of being and becoming and our lives continuously express possibility. However, we must give ourselves a chance to win by staying true to the Manufacturer's design and the box He created us for. If we have the courage to embrace the freedom of His limitation, we will truly go beyond anything we could have imagined.

Summary and Reflections

"We define potential as the 'possible as opposed to actual; capable of being or becoming and expressing possibility'."

Success is in the seed

"Everything needed to become is already within the seed, and given the chance, all the potential within that seed will grow into all it was designed to be."

Coached to cause

"Great coaches see the seed; they see what someone can become, because they understand what they are."

Fruit comes out of root

"When *truth* and *trust* form our root system, the outcome is fruit – God fruit – fruit that will not only last, but fruit that is an authentic expression of who we are and the God-box we live within!"

Some things are possible

"Accepting 'some things' is not defeatist – it's genius."

To help realise potential think about the following:

Who am I?

If you haven't already done so, why not take a personality profile. (In many cases these are free or incur a modest cost.)

What have I got?

If you haven't already done so, why not engage in a "strength-finders" assessment, which will help you to identity some of the areas you actually have passion and gift for.

Find a coach

Maybe all of this challenges you and you don't know where to start. Is there someone in your church, your church leadership or world who has the skills to coach you in the right direction? They may not be your coach for life or for everything, but they might just help to get you started.

Have a go!

Don't sit and wait for that magic moment. Engage in something that you like, that you seem to have the skills for and that enlarges and enriches you. Have a go and if you don't like it, try something else.

Footnotes:

1. Neymar: Brazil's humble superstar, BBC video article released on 4th July, 2014.
2. Article on Jade Jones on www.bbc.co.uk August 2012.
3. Andy Stanley, Visioneering, p.46

10
#HAPPYTIRED – FULFILMENT

#Happytired seems to be a contradiction, but in the context of what we're looking at, I believe it is a perfect combination – a little bit like the idea of #emptyfull, which we looked at in a previous chapter. Happiness in the God-box is not selfish or egocentric, but finds its energy around the epicentre of the will of God and the desire to please Him above all else. As we discover this life-transforming reality, it is only then that we as human beings find a happiness that transcends things and experiences, leading us to a place of inner contentment and joy.

As a child, I was taught in Sunday School that the definition of happiness was something that depended on "happenings". But the happiness, fulfilment and joy that I'm referring to in this chapter, is less to do with what is happening to us and more about how we are happening to the world around us. The happiness of happenings leaves me vulnerable to the ebb and flow of each new day (and moment within that day). It can leave me exposed to my moods and even the reactions of those around me (not that these are unimportant). However, happiness in the God-box is more about who God is, what God has said and, in turn, how we respond to that, thus helping to shape who we are and how we live. In this scenario, it is entirely possible that my happenings may not be pleasant, but my heart will be at peace. It may be that there is little to "make me happy", but yet I am happy.

I think Jesus illustrates this apparent contradiction brilliantly, when the writer to the Hebrews says,

"...who for the joy set before Him endured the cross, scorning its shame, and sat down at the right hand of the throne of God." (Hebrews 12:2)

Read this slowly and carefully and feel the paradox contained within this statement. There is little within this verse that would create happiness and yet Jesus is motivated by joy and lives a fulfilled and fruitful life. Within this one verse there are four key phrases I want us to dwell on, in order to dig under the surface. I believe these keys can empower and encourage us to live #happytired within the God-box.

"...who for the joy set before Him endured the cross, scorning its shame, and sat down at the right hand of the throne of God."

Though the word joy, *chaírō,* points to rejoicing and gladness, it is not a reference to self-indulgence, personal ambition or individual experience. Rather it is linked closely to the very next phrase, namely, "set before Him". The word *prókeimai* is delightful, being made up of two words, *pró* (before) and *keímai* (to be laid, set or lie before). Something is set or laid before Jesus and it's that something which is causing His joy. His joy is not random, coming from a happy personality type, His joy is coming from something He sees, something that now stands before Him. This is so important when it comes to an understanding of Jesus' joy. This is not the product of an "easy-go-lightly" attitude or a man breezing through life without a care in the world. It is the opposite. Jesus has joy because whatever has been set before Him He has chosen to engage with and do. The thing before Him is not only causing Him joy, it has become His joy!

So what has been set before Him?

Specifically, of course, we can reference the cross (and we'll look at this in just a minute), but I think it is bigger than that. I think what lies before Jesus is the purpose of God, the will of the Father, an understanding of what His Father wants and His delight in doing that and that alone. In a sense, the Father is putting a box in front of Jesus and asking Him to climb into it. Jesus knows that the box will involve the cross, shame, pain and a world He is yet to experience, but that's not His focus. Whatever the detail, He's made a decision based on what the Father wants and not what He would like, and with it has moved the epicentre of His happiness from what happens to Him to how *He happens to His world*.

If we can accept this radical yet simple truth to embrace whatever the Father sets before us, then we will always be happy in the biblical sense of the word and our inner world will be saturated with a joy that cannot be stolen, corrupted or tarnished by what is happening to us. Surrendering to whatever the Father has set before us ensures that we happen to our world. Happenings happen every day, but they can only dictate to us if our inner world has nothing with which to resist and overcome.

"...who for the joy set before Him endured the cross, scorning its shame, and sat down at the right hand of the throne of God."

The word translated "endured" here is fascinating. It's the word *hupoménō* and again is made up of two words, *hupó* (under) and *ménō* (to remain). The writer to the Hebrews, under the inspiration of the Spirit, deliberately chooses this word, pointing to the fact that Jesus remained under. Specifically, He remained under the cross – that is, He accepted the cross, took the cross, hung on the cross and died on the cross. However, generally it may point to the wider "set before" purpose of God, that whatever was set before Him by the Father, Jesus made a decision to remain under, no matter what. What a picture this is! Jesus remained under – or in the language of this book, Jesus stayed in the God-box and refused to leave it.

We must not confuse the idea of "remaining under" as somehow being overcome by His circumstances or being powerless to do anything. Jesus remains under not because He has to or because there is no other option. He remains under because He has made a decision to. He stays under as an act of His will.

Remaining under can be very difficult, especially when we feel the circumstances we're in are not what we'd like them to be, or we'd like to move from the place we're standing in. But there are moments when we must remain under, no matter what. If we know that what we're doing is the right thing, we're doing it in the right place, and we're doing it the way we believe God has asked of us, then we must remain under. If it becomes impossible for us to remain, that is something entirely different. Then I believe God will take care of the details outside of our control. But it is our responsibility not to climb out of the God-box or run from under the God-burden. Often we believe that if we can get out from under the pressure, then everything will be alright – and there may be moments when that is true – but what we must not get out from under is the will of God for our lives, because then wherever we go, we'll be experiencing second best, at best, and that will never make us happy!

When tempted to get out from under the moment we're in, ask yourself (or a trusted friend) the following questions:

- Did God bring me here? *(If so, then stay)*
- Am I doing what I believe God has asked of me? *(If yes, then keep doing it)*
- Can I do what He's asked me to do? *(If not, why not?)*
- Has God released me to go? *(If He has, you can't stay)*

We must not endure because of some martyr syndrome or a fear of failing. Instead, like Jesus, we must endure or stay under because we know it is the right thing to do, and until God permits otherwise or it becomes truly impossible for us to remain under, we must stay, endure and finish.

"...who for the joy set before Him endured the cross, scorning its shame, and sat down at the right hand of the throne of God."

The third phrase of note, "scorning its shame", comes out of the word *kataphronéō*, which breaks down into *kata* (against) and *phronéō* (to think). Thus it implies "to think against" or to hold something in contempt or even to despise it. Note again through this, the intentionality of Jesus. This is not random or the result of His personality shape, rather this is a decision to think a certain way about certain things. On a natural level, there was shame associated with His course of action, but Jesus chose to reject that thinking and think of the cross, specifically, and the purpose of God, generally, in a different way. He literally made His mind think in a scornful, dismissive way about the negative implications associated with the will of God. Wow!

Thinking certain thoughts doesn't come naturally. You and I must train our minds to think "right" about the right things. Paul urges us to allow our behaviour to be transformed by the "renewing of our minds" and that can only happen if we're prepared to grant God's truth access to our minds and authority over them. I love what Dr Caroline Leaf says in her book, *Who Switched Off My Brain*:

"Thoughts are measurable and occupy mental 'real estate'. Thoughts are active; they grow and change. Thoughts influence every decision, word, action and physical reaction we make."[1]

Our thoughts occupy "mental real estate" or what the Bible might term "strongholds" and through their occupation, our thoughts start to dictate our actions and behaviours. Though we can work hard at behavioural modification, the true route to transformation is by having our thinking processes revolutionised. When we think different we live different. Had Jesus allowed the mentality associated with the cross to drive His thinking He would have run a thousand miles in the opposite direction. Instead, He trained His mind to think differently about the cross and the purpose of the Father. He intentionally rejected the philosophy of His day and made His mind think a certain way. That's why He never lost His joy and never got lost on the journey.

As Caroline Leaf further concludes,

"Although you may not be able to control your environment all of the time, you can control how it affects your brain."[2]

Or, put another way in the context of this chapter, we cannot control what happens to us or around us, but we can make a decision that our happiness and joy isn't reliant on what happens to us, but how we happen to our world!

Let's connect the links we've identified so far.

Firstly, Jesus embraced what the Father set before Him. In fact, the purpose of the Father became His joy.

Secondly, Jesus stayed under the purpose set out for Him and refused to climb out of the God-box, even though it meant the cross.

Thirdly, Jesus thought in a specific way about the shame implications associated with the purpose of the Father, choosing to despise them and hold them so lightly that they had no grip on Him whatsoever!

This all adds up to a dynamic picture of Jesus. This is a man not allowing happenings to dictate to His happiness, but rather ensuring that who He is, what He's got and why He's here, is happening to His world. It is this mindset and process that produces the joy within Him and it is this that makes Him happy. He is able to sit with His disciples at the end of a long day #happytired.

"...who for the joy set before Him endured the cross, scorning its shame, and sat down at the right hand of the throne of God."

A whole book could be written on the imagery behind "sitting down", but in the context of Jesus' journey, it seems to point to three key ideas.

He had finished

This seems pretty obvious in the context. Remember, the writer to the Hebrews is trying to encourage a group of believers to stay the course and not quit, but finish their particular race. The writer shows that Jesus finished His race and therefore was able to sit down.

He was honoured

Jesus isn't given any old seat – He's now sitting at the right hand of the Father, and not on a throne beside His, but on the same throne, sharing the throne. There can be no higher place of honour for Jesus, put there by the Father.

He is given authority

Jesus now has a newly granted authority. We saw this in chapter five, specifically, where Jesus was given a name "above every name". Jesus is now able to move into a new realm of authority because He remained under the authority of the Father while on earth and finished what the Father put before Him. He went higher because He remained under!

Having accepted what was placed before Him, having remained under and within His Father's purpose for Him, having rejected any thinking that might distract Him from His cause, Jesus now enjoys the glory of finishing what He set out to do, the highest honour of the Father and an authority that only comes when one sits down. There are certain things we only get when we finish and stick with that which the Father asked of us. If we quit or run, or choose our own box, then although life can still be good, we will not and cannot have what the Father offered to Jesus.

All of this glorious theology is sandwiched by two very deliberate statements to us from the writer to the Hebrews. Let's look at them closely.

"Let us fix our eyes on Jesus…". This comes at the beginning of verse two, following on from the great chapter of faith where heroes of the faith are held up as our examples; people who by and large stayed within their God-box and did what God asked of them.

"Consider Him...". This comes at the beginning of verse three of the passage and builds on the incredible principles we've just glanced at.

Let's put the two phrases together, "...fix our eyes..." and "consider Him..."

Two very strong words bookend our four truths and I don't believe that this is a coincidence. The word translated "fix our eyes" is *aphoráō* and points to the idea of looking steadfastly and intently at something. This is not a passing glance, rather it is zoning in on one target and not allowing anything to distract us from it. The word translated "consider" is *analogízomai*, made up of *aná*, which in this case points to repetition and *logízomai* meaning to reckon and/or to think. Here our vision moves to thinking, to a position where we're considering something accurately and distinctly, not just once, but over and over again.

In the context of the passage this is incredible, but in the context of our subject material, of living in the freedom of limitation, of going beyond by staying within, of remaining within the God-box, this is unmissable. We are being urged to look at Jesus – and not just at Him, but how He lived, how He thought, the way He addressed Himself to the call of the Father – and we're being asked to do that over and over. To allow what we see (fix our eyes) to renew how we think (consider Him) and in turn transform the way we live – especially in the context of living in the God-box. These are principles for life in general, yes, but the writer to the Hebrews is pulling us down intentionally to this particular area. Jesus lived within the God-box, and how! See it, think about it and do it!

I love what Wayne Cordeiro said,

"Hope is a picture of a preferred future that does not diminish or tarnish with the changing moods of life."[3]

Happenings happen and, if we allow them to, they can dictate our purpose and thus our joy. But our joy is not dependent on what is going on around us, but on what is happening with us. If, like Jesus, we can settle the inner issues of laying down our lives for the greater purpose of the Father, then we won't just get joy from doing His will, His dream will become our joy.

To live within the God-box requires the courage to accept what the Father puts before us and the humility to live in it. It means making a decision to stay under when it would be the easiest thing in the world to get up and run in the opposite direction as fast as we can. To stay within the God-box demands that our minds align with how the Father thinks and not just how our world thinks. Staying within the God-box doesn't just happen and it won't just happen. We have to want it to happen and inevitably, though we have God's help, we have to make it happen. Just as Jesus did, so the writer to the Hebrews says we can.

We can allow the happenings around us to dictate our happiness and tell us what we must do and who we are – or we can settle the issue once and for all, place God at the centre, embrace what He has set before us, and ensure that the joy within us happens to our world. As we do so, at the end of each day we'll be able to smile at our world and tweet #happytired!

Summary and Reflections

"Happiness in the God-box is not selfish or egocentric, but finds its energy around the epicentre of the will of God and the desire to please Him above all else."

"... who for the joy set before Him endured the cross, scorning its shame, and sat down at the right hand of the throne of God."

"Remaining under can be very difficult, especially when we feel the circumstances we're in are not what we'd like them to be, or we'd like to move from the place we're standing in."

Perhaps you are in a tough situation and you want to know whether you should stay or go. Work through these questions:

Did God bring me here?
If God put you in the box, then stay!

Am I doing what I believe God has asked of me?
If yes, then keep doing it!

Can I do what He's asked me to do?
If not, why not?

Has God released me to go?
If He has, you can't stay!

"Hope is a picture of a preferred future that does not diminish or tarnish with the changing moods of life."

Footnotes:

1. Leaf, C., Who Switched Off My Brain, Thomas Nelson Publishers, 2009, p.13
2. Who Switched Off My Brain, p.53
3. Cordeiro W., Leading on Empty, Bethany House 2009, p.149

11
LIVING HIS DREAM — FREEDOM

"So Pharaoh sent for Joseph, and he was quickly brought from the dungeon. When he had shaved and changed his clothes, he came before Pharaoh." (Genesis 41:14).

This is a remarkable moment for a young man who arrived in Egypt as a slave at seventeen and spent most of his time up to this moment as a prisoner on a charge of attempted rape. As the prison door swings open, a thirty-year-old man emerges ready for the next stage of his journey. Joseph's journey has taken him from being a favoured son, through becoming a worthless slave and social scum (at least until now), and now here he stands in the courts of the most powerful man in Egypt, arguably the world, to become its saviour! What a life, what a journey, what a story.

Joseph goes from freedom to slavery to freedom again, but it might be argued that he learned to be truly free whilst a slave. The Joseph who stands before us now as a thirty-year-old is somewhat different from the seventeen-year-old we were first introduced to. Some might argue "time changes a man", but I don't believe that. Time just makes us older, not wiser. It wasn't the passage of time that changed Joseph. I believe he discovered something about God's purpose in the prison that he didn't understand as the favourite son and, having learned those lessons, when opportunity eventually came for the young Hebrew, he was ready to take it. It seems he's free on the inside, having learned that there is freedom in limitation – God's limitation!

My dream – my box

We have our first serious mention of Joseph in Genesis 37, where we learn a number of things about him immediately. His age (he's seventeen), his mentality (he brought a bad report to his father about his brothers – every man for himself), his status (his father loved him more than any of his other sons and made him a special coat as proof), his attitude (it's one thing to be given a special coat, it's another to wear it) and his standing (his brothers hated him).

All this in the first two verses of Joseph's story! From verses 5-11 we're then told that Joseph had two dreams. Though they are slightly different, they carry more or less the same message: "I am going to rise up and you lot are all going to serve me." So strong were his dreams that even his father saw fit to rebuke his favourite son.

What is interesting in these verses is that there is not one single reference to God. We tend to assume that God gave Joseph these dreams, and certainly the end of the story seems to back that theory up, but if you were reading this episode for the first time, you might be tempted to think that this is a young man with too much ego and too little brains! The dreams (wherever they have come from) are all about Joseph, what he will do, what he will become and how the world will treat him. At no point does he reference God as the author of the dreams or give God any credit that it may be His plan at work in and through all of this.

We sometimes excuse Joseph because he is only seventeen, but remember that in his culture he's long been a man. There were no "tweenagers" or teenagers in Joseph's day. One went from boyhood to manhood pretty quickly or one didn't do well. We sometimes get the impression that Joseph was young, soft, privileged and somewhat naïve, but in my opinion nothing could be further from the truth.

Joseph knew exactly what he was doing. He understood the politics of divided loyalties within his home and he worked them, most times to his advantage. He knew his brothers hated him, but he was the one with the favour, the coat and the dreams, and it would be a dark day indeed if any of them dared touch him.

I know this is difficult for many of you reading this chapter who may have read the story of Joseph yourself or heard it preached on many times. But do me a favour, read Genesis 37 from verses 2 to 11. Pretend that you've never heard of Joseph or what comes next and just let the text as it stands speak. If you do you'll discover as I have, these verses describe "my dream – my box".

At this moment at least, God is nowhere to be seen. The world is Joseph's oyster and he's the pearl! As a result, a number of dangerous things start to happen in and around Joseph, which eventually erupt into the darkest day of the family's history.

He's insular

We might find this a little uncomfortable, knowing who this young man becomes, but at this moment, looking on, we have a seventeen-year-old who has eyes only for himself. He might as well stand on a stage and shout to the world "Look at me!" Note the language of the dreams:

"Listen to this dream I had..." (v6)

"...my sheaf rose and stood upright..." (v7)

"...while your sheaves gathered round mine and bowed down to it." (v7)

"I had another dream..." (v9)

"...the sun, moon and eleven stars were bowing down to me." (v9)

Can you hear it? It's all about me ... and all this is for me ... look at me...

Wherever the dreams came from, Joseph's interpretation was clear and this created a dangerous place for him as it can for us. If we are not careful we start to believe that God is only there for us – to help us be everything we want to be, so that we can be successful and everyone can see how special we are. "After all, God loves me, wants the best for me, and He'll do everything to make me great!" we may think.

Though God's dream will involve us, it's not simply about us. His dream is bigger than any of us can even imagine, starting before the foundations of the world were set in place, and stretching on into eternity long after every clock has died of exhaustion. As big as we think our dreams are, they don't begin to scratch the surface of God's bigness on this issue.

Therefore, one of the most tragic things we can do is reduce the hugeness of God's dream down to our little world and our personal experience.

Joseph was about to discover that God doesn't fit into "I", and if we are to truly live free and touch the outer realms of God's plan for us, we must accept the reality that there is no "I" in God either! I love how Malcolm Duncan puts it in his book *Risk Takers*:

"The deepest flaw is that we put ourselves at the centre of the Great Story."[1]

He's insensitive

Before even a hint of a dream is presented, the story makes the feelings of his brothers very clear:

"...they hated him and could not speak a kind word to him." (v4)

I'm not always the sharpest tool in the box, but if I was Joseph I think I would have read these signals loud and clear! Joseph is not stupid, in fact he is a highly intelligent young man and his later experiences also demonstrate his emotional intelligence. So what happens next can only be because of a calculated, intentional decision. He inflames an already tense situation with his first dream ... and the reaction?

"...they hated him all the more." (v5)

Now there's a shock.

But still he continues in sharing the second dream:

"And they hated him all the more because of his dream and what he had said." (v8)

Joseph doesn't care, that's the only conclusion. He's so caught up with the excitement of what he's going to become that he doesn't really care about his brothers' feelings or reactions. After all, they will be bit-players in his show! Joseph even demonstrates a disregard for his father, a massive issue in Hebrew and eastern culture even back then. He doesn't spare his father's feelings by letting him know that one day he will bow down too!

Insensitivity to others is the surest sign we're living our own dream and not God's. We've all made mistakes by saying inappropriate things or by doing the wrong thing at the wrong time, but that's not what I'm talking about. This goes beyond an occasional mistake, rather it's a mind set, a heart-scape that is totally selfish; that sees those around us as subservient to our dream and our role.

He's isolated

Eventually Joseph ends up down a hole without a friend in the world, save Reuben, and I suspect the only reason Reuben stood up for him was because he was the first born and he was thinking of the heartbreak it will cause his father.

"Reuben said this to rescue him from them and take him back to his father." (v22)

Joseph is friendless. No one stands up for him, no one cares for him, no one truly loves him and no one believes in him.

"Then we'll see what becomes of his dreams." (v20)

It stands to reason, if we interpret life through an insular mind set, that we naturally become desensitised to the needs, wants and dreams of others around us. The only realistic outcome is isolation! The tragedy is that we don't really know we're isolated until we're in a position where we need someone to stand up for us and there's no one there. How horrible it must have been for Joseph to hear his brothers discussing whether he should live or die. What a nightmare to be sold as a slave without a single objection raised. Food for thought on the road to Egypt!

"My dream – my box" wasn't working for Joseph and I'm

pretty sure it won't work for us either.

Broken dream – Potiphar's box

It is fascinating that the first reference to God in Joseph's story is as a slave in Egypt. The Captain of Pharaoh's guard bought the Hebrew slave and the story reveals,

"The Lord was with Joseph and he prospered..." (Genesis 39:2)

In fact, we go from zero to five references about the Lord in the space of as many verses. We might want to have a debate on whether it was actually God's will for Joseph to be a slave in Potiphar's house or not, but one thing is for sure, God was there. God was *so* there that Potiphar recognised it and placed Joseph in charge of his whole household. Joseph found himself in an unimaginable box, but God was there with him, working in him, for him, with him and through him.

Serving Joseph

It is surely no coincidence that alongside the references to the Lord at work, Joseph also starts to go to work himself and soon his skills are clear for all to see. Joseph stands out from the crowd even as a slave and the true leader within him starts to emerge. He serves with such excellence that he is promoted within Potiphar's house. Life is as good as it gets for a slave.

"...with Joseph in charge, he did not concern himself with anything except the food he ate." (Genesis 39:6)

Selfless Joseph

Potiphar's wife took a fancy to the young man, however, and relentlessly tried to get him to have sex with her, but he refused.

As the chief attendant, Joseph could have made an affair work, since he was in charge of staff rotas and could ensure he and the lady of the house had all the time they needed. But he refused. However, though I admire his refusal at such continuous sexual provocation, I'm more in awe of his reasoning:

"With me in charge, my master does not concern himself with anything in the house; everything he owns he has entrusted to my care. No one is greater in this house than I am. My master has withheld nothing from me, except you, because you are his wife. How then could I do such a wicked thing and sin against God?" (Genesis 39:8-9)

Note the change in thinking and language. As a seventeen-year-old in his father's house, his position was privileged and all too often he interpreted this as an opportunity for self-promotion. Now, his position is seen as service and becomes an opportunity to selflessly protect his master. Joseph isn't thinking of himself, he's now starting to think of how others feel, the impact of his actions on another man's world. In this new box, Joseph isn't at the centre, Potiphar is, and Joseph gives himself to serving his master wholeheartedly.

What a change is starting to take place. What has happened to the man who was telling on his brothers, issuing edicts, wearing the colours of favour and talking about himself? What has happened to the man who expected everyone to serve him? It seems this new, uncomfortable box, helped by the active presence of God is bringing out the best in our young hero to be. In restriction and limitation, Joseph is beginning to find freedom.

Lost dream – prison box

Just when everything seemed to be going well, Joseph finds

himself on a dirty prison floor, lucky to have escaped with his life. Potiphar's wife didn't like being repulsed by a slave, so she accused the young man of attempted rape and probably expected him to die a horribly painful death. But no! Though Potiphar was angry, it wasn't enough to have Joseph executed. This makes no sense. In prison, Joseph was of no value to Potiphar; none of his investment would be realised by keeping him there, so why not have him executed and be done with it He was, after all, only a slave. For whatever reason, and I have my theories, Joseph ends up in prison:

"...the place where the king's prisoners were confined." (Genesis 39:20)

It's here that we read these words again:

"...the Lord was with him..." (Genesis 39:21)

With the combination of the Lord's presence and Joseph's skill, he again gets a promotion within the prison and we read almost identical words of those previously heard in Potiphar's house:

"The warder paid no attention to anything under Joseph's care..." (Genesis 39:23)

The boy with the richly ornamented coat could never have imagined in his wildest dreams that he would end up in a place like this. But here he is, in the warden's box and it seems the dream has well and truly gone. But no, even in this seemingly terrible box, God is with him and who he is continues to emerge.

Joseph the leader

Look at these statements:

"...the warder put Joseph in charge of all those held in the prison and he was made responsible for all that was done there."

(Genesis 39:22)

This didn't happen because Joseph was good looking or because he'd mastered the art of making other people feel good. It happened because the warder (remember, if prisoners escape or die unexpectedly he has to "pay") saw serious leadership ability in the young Hebrew, who was probably between 19-20 years old when he entered prison. The warder is not naïve or stupid, he isn't going to risk his career on an unproven boy. But he promotes Joseph because he sees clear, obvious, productive leadership gifts at work, and he would be silly not to promote him. At work is the combination of God-given wisdom (Acts 8:10) and God-given gifts. But Joseph had to use them both. I believe the gifts now being demonstrated in the prison he had from birth and had as a young man at home, but it's only now, in a situation where he is almost forced to act, that he starts to truly use them, and oh how they shine!

Our God-given gifts don't need a special moment to shine and operate, they just need to be let loose. The best place for them to shine is the place where people least expect it, so when they do, everyone notices. It would have been easy for Joseph to hide his talents whilst seeing out his time in prison, but no, instead he saw the prison box as an opportunity and decided to take it with all his might. Had he not been so forthcoming with his leadership gifts, then the next part of the story might not have happened. It was his willingness to serve as a leader that created the opportunity for him to "see" once again as a dreamer!

Joseph the dreamer

For some reason of displeasure, Pharaoh's Butler (chief cupbearer) and Baker were sent to prison and handed over to the Captain of the Guard. The next few words are crucial:

"The captain of the guard assigned them to Joseph, and he attended them." (Genesis 40:4)

Don't miss that moment, it's an incredible thought. Joseph received these two men into his care because he had excelled as a leader. That in turn opened the door for Joseph's other supernatural God-given gift to excel – that of interpreting dreams. Without the former, the latter would have been lost!

You can read the story for yourself, but essentially, the two men have dreams and they're disturbed by them. Note the following:

"...he saw that they were dejected..." (v6)

"Why are your faces so sad today?" (v7)

"Do not interpretations belong to God? Tell me your dreams." (v8)

Spot the differences? What a change from the young man we first met. He notices how dejected these men are. He enquires after their well being and when he offers them a solution, it is a God-inspired, God-given one. This is no longer about him. That has changed. Now it's about them and ultimately about Him! Joseph is changing. He's starting to understand that although he's in a box, a literal box of prison, he doesn't have to be limited or restricted in what he can be or do. Joseph had every right to ignore these men and let them wallow in their own self-pity, but instead, as a leader, he steps in and, as a dreamer, he brings the supernatural to the routine, mundane, murky world of prison.

Joseph the keeper

Not only did Joseph interpret their dreams (good news for the butler, not so good for the baker), but within three days his words came to pass. All Joseph asked was that the cupbearer "mention him" to Pharaoh. Easy right? But the text drops a boom moment at the end of this episode:

"The chief cupbearer, did not remember Joseph; he forgot him." (Genesis 40:23)

How does that happen? How do you forget someone like Joseph? Yet he did and not just for a few moments, but for two whole years! The text is silent on the gap between 40:23 and 41:1, save the passing of time, but it seems to me (though I can't strictly prove this) that Joseph kept doing what he was doing during that time. Joseph kept attending to the prisoners, he kept serving the warden and he kept showing up every day of those two long, difficult years.

Joseph has changed. Joseph can now begin to see something bigger. The gifts he started to flirt with as a seventeen-year-old, he is not only supremely comfortable with, but extraordinarily efficient with. During those two years, Joseph continues to serve, lead, grow and dream, so that one day, a day that began like any other day, something extraordinary happened and he was ready to take his opportunity.

"So Pharaoh sent for Joseph, and he was quickly brought from the dungeon. When he had shaved and changed his clothes, he came before Pharaoh." (Genesis 41:14).

God's dream – God's box

Thirteen years after hobbling into Egypt in chains, Joseph becomes an overnight success. Though the prison door opened suddenly, Joseph was ready to serve because he had been ready for a long time. I love how Stephen puts it in Acts:

"He [God] gave Joseph wisdom and enabled him to gain the goodwill of Pharaoh king of Egypt; so he made him ruler over

Egypt and all his palace." (Acts 8:9-10)

I love the combination that's captured here of God-given wisdom, favour and gifts all at work to conspire to a glorious moment of destiny. Joseph becomes the custodian of an extraordinary set of circumstances, one honed in thirteen years of living within restriction, while at the same time not succumbing to limitation. Joseph is ready and through his superb leadership gifts, Egypt and the surrounding nations are saved, including his own.

Some twenty-two years later after selling him as a slave, Joseph's brothers turn up and Joseph eventually reveals himself to them. It must have been a shocking moment for all involved. But not as much as the language of Joseph and the reassurance he gives to his brothers:

"...to save lives God sent me ahead of you." (Genesis 45:5)

"But God sent me ahead of you to preserve for you a remnant on earth and to save your lives by a great deliverance." (v7)

"...it was not you who sent me here, but God." (v8)

"He made me father to Pharaoh..." (v8)

"God has made me lord of Egypt..." (v9)

"I will provide for you there..." (v11)

Compare this language to the speech we heard from the seventeen year old. Back then the dream was his and it was all about him. Now, the dream is God's and it is all about them.

Every time he mentioned himself back them it was about him. Every time he mentions himself now, it's in reference to either what God has done for him or what he is about to do through him.

I love this. Joseph has moved from "my dream – my box" to "God's dream – God's box". He's come to understand that his life is not actually about him, but about God's purpose and God's people. Though he seems to have encountered more restriction in Egypt, he's now freer than he was as a seventeen-year-old. Had Joseph been left to his own devices, he would have been a prisoner in his father's coloured coat, but without it he had to find God, find himself and find the true meaning of his God-given dreams. When he stands before his brothers and says, "I am Joseph" (v3) he's not waiting to be served by them, but he's now one who longs to serve them. Where he once thought that his dream was about them serving him, as a man of God he has now discovered that his dream was about him serving and saving them! In the box of God's purpose, Joseph has become a bigger man than would ever have been possible had he stayed the favourite son of his father.

It's easy to read the story of Joseph from the finish and know it all works out in the end. Okay, he had a few bumps on the road, but he eventually made it and it all worked out. But closer examination of the story shows us that in chapter 37, as a seventeen-year-old, Joseph thought he was free when he was actually trapped by his own arrogance and smallness. The self-centred coloured coat-wearing boy was in danger of blowing his God-given destiny out of the water. Once the coat came off, the true God-shaped Joseph started to emerge in the most unlikely contexts. God was with Joseph in the box of Potiphar's house and the box of prison, but ironically it was within these boxes that Joseph the leader, the dreamer and the keeper truly emerged.

Joseph teaches us a powerful lesson. The world in which we feel big can, if we're not careful, actually become small if that world is about us, our dreams, our lives and our desires. The "coat" may look good, but it may actually be restricting our movement and jeopardising our future. God had more for Joseph beyond the coat and more beyond his narrow interpretation of his dreams. Your dream may feel big to you, but trust me, His dream for you is much, much bigger and better. His route may not be the pathway you want to walk on, but if you trust Him, not only will He get you to your destination but He'll be with you every step of the way. If we dare to dream God's dream and live in God's box, rather than restriction we'll find freedom and the box that He puts us in will be much, much bigger than anything we thought possible ... just ask Joseph.

Summary and Reflections

"The deepest flaw is that we put ourselves at the centre of the Great Story."[2]

A self-centred interpretation of God's dream for our life will always produce at least 3 things (as it did in the life of Joseph):

Insular

"...one of the most tragic things we can do is reduce the hugeness of God's dream down to our little world and our personal experience."

Is your box or dream insular? Is it only about self-promotion, and/or is it obsessed with what God can do for you?

Insensitive

"Insensitivity to others is the surest sign we're living our own dream and not God's."

Does your box or dream involve the encouragement, promotion, releasing and blessing of others? Is it more about what others can do for you, or about what you can do for them?

Isolated

"The tragedy is that we don't really know we're isolated until we're in a position where we need someone to stand up for us and there's no one there."

Does your box or dream require the help of others to make it happen, or is it just down to your individual brilliance?

Don't cling on to a man-made coat – rather grab hold of a God-ordained cause.

Footnotes:

1. Duncan, M., Risk Takers – Living as God Intended, Monarch Books, 2013 p.79

2. Ibid.

12
LIMITS DON'T MEAN LIMITATION

From the previous chapter we can safely conclude that Joseph lived an incredible life. He journeys from the favoured son with a special coat to the slave of Potiphar, to the attendant of the prison warder, and eventually arrives as the Prime Minister of Egypt. Through that journey he keeps his faith, holds his nerve and somehow, with the help of God, sees his dreams become a reality. In the process he is not only instrumental in saving his own people, but many nations of the known world. Joseph's life story is truly amazing. So when the writer to the Hebrews is trying to think of a particular aspect of his life to mention in the "roll call of faith" in Hebrews 11, one might think his biggest challenge will be what to leave out! There is so much of faith about Joseph's life and so much that could enrich this great passage. So what does the writer give us?

"By faith Joseph, when his end was near, spoke about the Exodus of the Israelites from Egypt and gave instructions about his bones." (Hebrews 11:22)

That's it? That's all we're going to get about one of the greatest characters in the Old Testament? I'm afraid so, but before we rush off in disgust we should consider why this statement, of all possible statements about Joseph, is the one that the writer decides to include. There must be some greater significance about what is going on here than meets the eye. Surely Joseph's life adds up to more than faith concerning his burial arrangements?

The reference in Hebrews relates directly to Joseph's final recorded words in Genesis:

"God will surely come to your aid, and then you must carry my bones up from this place." (Genesis 50:25)

The writer to the Hebrews is alluding to Joseph's final words because they contain and confess faith that we need to understand. The final image we have of Joseph in Genesis is given to us in the very next verse:

"And after they embalmed him, he was placed in a coffin in Egypt." (Genesis 50:26)

The last statement of Joseph's life in Genesis is that he is placed in a box, but before that happens, his confession and request ensure that his faith, vision, passion and expectation is not limited to that box. His body may reside in a coffin, but the dream, God's dream, lives on and he still wants to be part of it. Joseph's faith statement, captured for us in Hebrews, echoing his final words, is a confession over the coffin; a declaration that even from the restriction of this final box, there are no limitations to the purpose of God. From the grave he declares that we can still go beyond by staying within and that limits don't mean limitation!

So what does Joseph's confession teach us when we're

thinking about our own lives, the box we're in and the influence we desire for the glory of God?

My end is not The End

Apparently W.C. Fields was caught reading a Bible as he approached death. The surprised person asked why he was reading it and he replied, "I'm looking for a loophole."

In the words we read about Joseph he's not looking for a loophole, he's looking for an opportunity. Most people on their deathbed have a tendency to look back on their lives, but not Joseph. He's not looking back, he's looking forward. Though Joseph knows that his earthly existence is about to come to an end, the purposes and plans of God are still secure and alive. Joseph understands that his end is not The End! Whatever his personal limits now are, he has come to the place of faith that his limits are not placing any limitation upon God and what He can do. As Joseph's active living part comes to an end, he has full confidence in the multi-generational God who can and will do that which He has purposed, even after Joseph has gone.

When we are in the middle of our journey it is easy to fall into the trap that somehow it all depends on us. How would my family cope without me? How would my church survive if I was no longer their leader? How will things turn out if I'm not around? Our role is important, of course, and the premise of this book has been to help us see how important it is and have the courage to live within the boundaries of our role and God-given box. But we must not burden ourselves with God-stuff, with the things that only God can do. To try and carry this will place us under unbearable pressure, drive us to insecurity and push us to believe our own PR – that somehow, we are indispensable and that it won't be the same without us. The truth is, it won't be the same without us, but it won't stop either! When Joseph died the world kept spinning, the sun kept shining, and once they had embalmed him and placed him in a coffin ... they moved on with life. We're important, but we're not indispensable!

Indispensability flows out of insecurity, which has its foundation in a life and mind set that tries to live outside the God-designed box for our lives. When we try to do everything, when we believe we can be all things to all people, and when we live outside the boundaries, then we create a world that needs us (although really, we need it) and therefore can't live without us. The irony is that such a mind set disempowers our world and shrinks our influence. It doesn't grow us, rather it ultimately diminishes us.

As brilliant as Joseph was, he died and life moved on. Joseph had the foresight and wisdom to understand this, hence he prepared his family and his nation not only for the moment of his death, but for life beyond his death. Joseph didn't want them focusing on him, rather he wanted them focused on Him, the One true and Living God.

Our end, of course, does not just refer to death. Our end can be the limit of our influence, the moment we have to let go, the finishing of a season in life, the conclusion of a ministry opportunity or the end of something/someone we have invested in.

The danger is, we think because we stop, it stops; that because we're not there and directly involved that now, somehow, it's over. But Joseph teaches us that even when we can no longer contribute, our influence and legacy can live on and empower. Our limits don't necessarily mean limitation!

Don't fall into the trap of believing it all depends on you

It doesn't! You're important, you're special and you're unique, but you're not God. His purpose is bigger than us all and although we have an important role within it, we are not it. God was running the universe before we were born and He'll continue to do it after we've gone.

Don't fall into thinking that it all ends with you

It doesn't! Our unique contribution may end at that season, or in a particular moment, but that doesn't signal The End. Those words and that authority lie in the hands of Almighty God alone. He started it and He will finish it. It is our job to do our bit and leave the rest to Him.

God gets the final word

Note Joseph's words:

"I am about to die. But God will surely come to your aid and take you up out of this land to the land He promised on oath to Abraham, Isaac and Jacob." (Genesis 50:24)

"God will surely come to your aid..." (v25)

Joseph's confidence in God's ability to deliver comes from the promise God has made, a promise that roots his people to a land of their own. Twice he repeats his conviction that, "God will surely come to your aid" because he is sure that God will do what He said He would do. Their eventual restriction will become God's opportunity to demonstrate His power and majesty, and whatever happens they must trust that what He said He would do! Such was his confidence, that instead of allowing his body to receive the pomp and ceremony afforded to such an influential official, Joseph opts to have his body embalmed and placed in a coffin (somewhere), until the day God showed up to deliver them.

Four hundred years later, Moses showed up and eventually, after a struggle, the people, Joseph's people, were allowed to leave Egypt and journey to their own land promised to them by God. In the midst of the excitement of exodus, tucked away in the text is a lovely statement.

"Moses took the bones of Joseph with him because Joseph had made the sons of Israel swear an oath. He had said, 'God will surely come to your aid, and then you must carry my bones with you up from this place.'" (Exodus 13:19)

Wow! Look at those words closely. They are almost word for word as spoken by Joseph. It seems that Joseph's conviction made such an impact on his generation that not only was his coffin preserved, but his words were too. In fact, I would argue that it is his words not his body that are making the journey to the land of promise! It took four hundred years, and in truth, it would take another 40 or so before Joseph's bones actually came to rest in the land of promise, but this event demonstrates that Joseph had been resting in God's promise long before he died.

Joseph's faith in the promise of God is remarkable for two reasons.

Firstly, he wasn't there when the promise was given.

What he's confessing is something that has been given to him by somebody else. At some point on his journey, Joseph may have had an experience with God where God repeated this same promise, but there's nothing on record that would prove that. So if we assume that didn't happen, then Joseph believes a promise given to someone else before he was even born.

Secondly, he wasn't there when the promise was fulfilled.

Joseph wasn't going to see to the outworking of the promise because he was about to die. Therefore it would have been so easy for him not to care. "Well, if I'm not going to get to see it, why should I be bothered?" But Joseph did care, because a long time before that he came to the conclusion that God's purpose and promise to him wasn't just about or for him, but rather God's plan was much, much bigger than any one individual.

What do we learn from this?

The revelation of Abraham, Isaac and Jacob became his revelation and even though he wouldn't see the fulfilment of the promise with his eyes, he saw it in his heart. Joseph's confession came out of revelation and that alone was the source of his confidence. Joseph occupies possibly the hardest place in any journey, the "inbetweener", having not been there at the beginning and he won't be there at the end. Yet he lives with faith, vision, courage and conviction. He will not allow those details to dictate to him or limit him. Though he is about to enter a box, God's promise will not be chained or contained by that box.

Whatever box we are in, it is important to remember, "the word of God is not chained" (2 Timothy 2:9). Joseph's bones lay in a coffin for hundreds of years, but God's promise wasn't in the coffin with him. God's word was at work, preparing the moment for one of the greatest exoduses in history and the glorious fulfilment of a long awaited promise. Whatever the limits we find ourselves in, that does not bring limitation to the promise of God, which works on our behalf whether we feel it or not or see it or not!

Perhaps there were moments when people in Egypt would doubt the promise, and perhaps they would make their way to Joseph's coffin and encourage themselves, "God will come ... one day." Approximately ten generations passed before God showed up, but He did, and Joseph's bones were ready to go, just like he was ready to go when the prison door swung open.

God's promise to us, for us and through us, is bigger than the limits we feel we may be in right now. It is our responsibility to hold onto those promises, confess them and keep believing that what God has spoken, He will do – even when they look as dead as an embalmed Joseph in his coffin. If God has spoken it, He can do it and He will do it. In truth, we're not always sure when He will do it or how He will do it, but like Joseph we must come to the unshakable conviction ... *He will do it!*

When it comes to the promise of God in your life, remember the following:

Revelation fuels our reality!

Joseph heard something for himself that he didn't hear first hand, yet it became real to him and dictated his own reality. Our beliefs dictate our behaviour and ultimately determine the reality we live in. We see the world not always as it is, but we always see the world as we are. How we are, how we think, the convictions we hold, are the revelations that determine our reality. As a person thinks, so they are – at least to them!

Joseph was about to enter his final box, but the revelation that pulsated within him meant that he would go beyond, even though he had to stay within.

The truth always trumps facts!

The facts weren't looking good for Joseph personally and later the facts got significantly worse for the nation. A new Pharaoh arose who didn't know Joseph and his people were oppressed and persecuted. The facts screamed impossibility, but the embalmed body in the coffin kept confessing, "God will come to your aid." God's truth ultimately triumphs over human facts, because God's word is greater than any human circumstance, obstacle or scheme.

When truth reigns in our hearts, whatever the limits, God's word is not chained and can work beyond our limitations. God's word, once spoken, will come to pass and will find a way to work through and in the circumstances to bring about God's purpose. The facts may scream limits, but the promise of God confesses that He will do what He has said He will do, and that reaches beyond any box.

When we see it before we see it, we've seen it!

At this point, Joseph hadn't seen or touched the land of promise for 93 years, and his bones wouldn't rest in the land for approximately another 450 years. Yet Joseph spoke as a man who could see it as if he were looking at it through his window. Though he would not see it, he saw it.

What an inspiration this must have been to his brothers. Maybe that's why his words are so accurately remembered all those years later. On his deathbed Joseph isn't looking back, or in, or down or around, rather Joseph is looking forward, his eyes focused on the prize, his confession steadfast. At 110 years old he could see the promise of God!

When we *see* something in our hearts then we have seen it. Whether we get to experience it directly and personally is another matter, but the fact that we can see it, means we can live in it now, even though it is not yet. Only God knows how the promises He has made to us will be fulfilled for us, but what we must not do is box the promises up so that they can only work our way. Rather, let's be like Joseph, who would have loved to have returned alive to the land of promise, his land, but that was not to be – yet, it did not prevent him from seeing it, living in it and investing in those who would one day get to do what he had longed to do.

In our first church, God gave me a promise that we would enter a new building debt free. I believed that promise would be fulfilled a certain way and I would be part of it, but in truth it was fulfilled in a completely different way, and someone else had the joy of seeing it fulfilled. The challenge I had was continuing to celebrate the promise even though it was working out a different way to that which I wanted or expected. Such thinking does more to box me up that any box I'm in. I've learned not to "box in" the promises of God, but rather let God do things the way He wants to do them, regardless of how that looks or works for me. When we see it before we see it, we'll always go beyond any boundary we're in.

God's box is always bigger than we think

Eventually, the people of God got through their wilderness experience and, under the leadership of Joshua, they entered the land of promise. Within the book of Joshua we have our final reference to Joseph's bones.

"And Joseph's bones, which the Israelites had brought up from Egypt, were buried at Shechem in the tract of land that Jacob bought for a hundred pieces of silver from the sons of Hamor, the father of Shechem. This became the inheritance of Joseph's descendants." (Joshua 24:32)

Immediately we see the multi-generational link within this verse. In Genesis 33 we are told that Jacob, Joseph's father returned to the land after a period of exile and the first thing he did after meeting Esau was to buy some land at Shechem. This was a significant act by Jacob (now called Israel), because he is claiming a stake in the land God promised and like his grandfather and father before him, he is literally investing in the promise by putting his own money into it. Even though the land has been promised to him, he buys it anyway. Jacob becomes an "owner" of the promise and now has a personal stake in it.

Jacob then built an altar there and called it, "El Elohe Israel" publicly establishing a confession: *El is the God of Israel*. Now remember, this is the first mention of Israel in the new land and the only time this particular confession is used and it's probable that Jacob is referring to himself – that God is the God of Israel (Jacob). So on this new plot of ground, Jacob builds an altar to God and names it in this very specific way. In this hugely significant moment, Jacob was not simply claiming land for himself, but for God. He was declaring in no uncertain terms, "I am God's man and this, my land, is now His land."

Jacob's land of course automatically becomes an inheritance for his children, but as we fast-forward the bones of Joseph are now returning. Where do they go? They are returned to the ancestral land of Jacob, placed on the site the patriarch first bought, on the site he built his first post-exile altar and on the site at which Israel, the name the nation would ultimately take, was first mentioned. Joseph's bones come to rest on this significant place. Once they do, the plot Jacob bought immediately becomes an inheritance not for Joseph but for Joseph's descendants! Thus Joseph's bones connect the past to the future, an act that would not have been possible had Joseph 450 years earlier, not insisted that his bones be taken with them. Jacob's faith (in buying the land) became an inheritance for Joseph and Joseph's faith (through his bones) became an inheritance for his descendants.

Suddenly what seems like a relatively small box takes on a much bigger, dynamic significance. Jacob and Joseph's actions seem so relatively insignificant in themselves, but when connected together something incredible starts to happen. When Jacob bought the land he could not have imagined the scenario hundreds of years later, and when Joseph gave orders about his bones, he could not have envisaged the outcome of Shechem. But somehow, they connect.

Out of these events there are some dynamic lessons to learn and remember.

God's box is so much bigger

We think our plans are big, but they are nothing compared to what God is into. Stand outside at night and look up at the myriad stars in our seen universe and we feel small, inadequate and awed – and so we should. For all our sophistication and genius, nothing compares to what He has done or is doing. Every now and again we need to gain perspective – that we're only human, living in relatively small boxes and given a relatively short time to leave a mark. We get caught up in the milliseconds of our lives and our achievements and we think we've cracked it, we've got it, we understand. Then we look at the stars and realise that however big we think we've made it, it's all so small.

That's why we've got to let God into our world and thinking, so that He can unlock our small minds and show us something much, much bigger than anything and everything we think is important.

We get consumed with our box; we think it's the most important thing in the world and we get precious about protecting and defending it. But in the midst of our box, we need to look up, look out and look forward, and allow the God of heaven to fill our eyes with faith and vision for something much bigger than we could have dreamed. Abraham had no heir, yet God said his descendants would be as the stars and the sand. His job was to produce "one heir", and it was God's job to do the rest – and what a job He's done. Abraham could not have imagined how his offspring of faith have prospered today, and all from that one boy.

We do the living and let Him do the connecting

When Jacob bought the land at Shechem, Joseph was just a young boy. Never in his wildest dreams could he have designed the scenario we've just witnessed. When Joseph gave the command about his bones Jacob was long dead and Egypt was home. He could not have thought that the circle would close again, but it did, and how.

It's not our job to work it out; it's our job to do the work. Don't concern yourself with how the threads will come together or how God will make it happen. Rather, concentrate your heart and mind on doing what is before you, so that however God works it out, you and I will have ensured that we played our part, we did what we could and we lived our moment of the story well.

My father became a Christian when he was 10 years old, the first of his family (aside from his mother). His father, my grandfather, came back from the Second World War probably suffering from some sort of post traumatic stress, but in those days men took off their uniforms, put on their civilian clothes and went back to work. That's what my grandfather did. Except that he started drinking heavily, he was a chain-smoker, he would gamble on two flies going up a wall and he was handy with his fists. For just over ten years after the war, his life gradually unravelled and threatened his world and everyone in it. My father started praying for my grandfather, three times a day, for over three years. Eventually (and it is a remarkable conversion story), my grandfather got saved. From the moment of his conversion he never smoked again, never drank, fought or gambled again. He was radically transformed. Thirty years later, my grandfather was walking down the street when he had the one and only vision of his life. Right there in the middle of the street God presented a vision before his eyes, outlining a number of things.

So powerful was it that my grandfather immediately asked to see the leaders of the church and told them what he had seen, one element of which particularly affected me. In his vision my grandfather had been told about my future and that the church had to send me to Bible College to prepare for that future. The rest, as they say, is history.

I love this story because it echoes the bones of Joseph. My father prayed for his father to become a Christian before I was born. My grandfather became a Christian and was directly instrumental in confirming the call of God I was feeling inside, and for my leaving for Bible College. My future was actually in the prayers of my father for his father. My dad could never have imagined that his prayers for his dad would actually impact the future of his unborn son. He just did what he did – and God did the rest! It's our responsibility to live the dots and it's God's responsibility to connect them.

As we draw this book to a close, don't be afraid of the God-box. If you will have the courage to stay within, you'll go beyond. If you have the faith to walk within God's limitation, then you'll live in freedom. If you will walk in His ways, He will sketch a world of possibility and opportunity for you and yours that in your wildest dreams, you never thought possible. Reject the #BigBoxMyth. We're all in boxes; the trick is discovering which box God wants us in and having the courage and confidence to live within it all the days of our lives. If we do, we'll go further in life and, even in death, our bones will speak.

I will not die an unlived life.
I will not live in fear of falling or catching fire.
I choose to inhabit my days, to allow my living to open me,
To make me less afraid, more accessible,
To loosen my heart until it become a wing, a torch, a promise.
I choose to risk my significance,
To live so that which came to me as seed goes to the next as blossom,
And that which came to me as blossom, goes on as fruit.[1]

Summary and Reflections

"The last statement of Joseph's life in Genesis is that he is placed in a box, but before that happens, his confession and request ensure that his faith, vision, passion and expectation is not limited to that box. His body may reside in a coffin, but the dream, God's dream, lives on and he still wants to be part of it."

My end is not The End

"Indispensability flows out of insecurity, which has its foundation in a life and mindset that tries to live outside the God-designed box for our lives."

What principles and practicalities can we build into our lives that protect us from a mentality of indispensability?

God gets the final word

"Joseph occupies possibly the hardest place in any journey, the 'inbetweener', having not been there at the beginning and he won't be there at the end."

Remind yourself of the promises that God has made to you specifically about your life, family, purpose and future. Write those words down, confess the promises in prayer, make them the bedrock of your faith and vision. Whatever it looks like, remember that "the word of God is not chained".

God's box is always bigger than we think

"We get caught up in the milliseconds of our lives and our achievements and we think we've cracked it, we've got it, we understand. Then we look at the stars and we realise that however big we think we've made it, it's all so small."

It is important to remember the bigness of God's plan and purposes. Look up and see the heavens filled with stars and understand your place in all of this. God's plan is not about you (though you are vital, special, unique and important), rather it is about the whole of the universe, in which He sits at the centre of which you are a part. Step back, look up and live big.

Footnotes:

1. Waldock, T., To plant a Walnut Tree, Nicolas Brealey Publishing, 2011, poem by Dawna Markova, p.71.

ABOUT THE AUTHOR

John was brought up in a Christian family just off the Shankill Road in Belfast, Northern Ireland, where at the age of eight he came to faith in Jesus. At sixteen he received a very clear call from God and went to Mattersey Hall Bible College, where he studied for three years. In 1987 he pioneered a work in Yorkshire for just over 9 years, before becoming senior leader of the Hub Christian Community in Rotherham for fifteen years. In September 2012 he took up a leadership post at Renewal Christian Centre, Solihull, where he served until the end of 2014. As a leader/teacher, John continues to empower and inspire leaders and the local church.

John is married to Dawn and they have three children, Elaina,

Simeon and Beth-Anne (not forgetting their beloved sausage dog, Pepperoni!)

John has a Masters degree in Pentecostal and Charismatic studies through Sheffield University, a PhD from the University of Wales, and has written ten books.

John's hobbies include supporting his beloved football team, Liverpool, listening to music, reading and watching great movies. He loves to eat and among his favourite food groups are Chinese, Italian and chocolate! When taking time out, John can be found in a local coffee shop enjoying a good book.

2:52 Learning To Grow on Purpose

As Jesus is about to enter into eighteen years of obscurity, Luke gives us only one clue as to His preoccupation during those years, informing us, "And Jesus grew in wisdom and stature, and in favour with God and man." (Luke 2:52)

The temptation is to think that Jesus grew "naturally" in these areas, but the verse implies that Jesus grew intentionally and deliberately. Jesus grew on purpose. It is tempting only to examine Jesus' miracle-laden ministry, His teaching, His death and resurrection – to look forward at what is about to happen, not look back at what has been. For approximately 3 years Jesus impacted His world, but these 3 years represent only 9% of His life on earth. What about the other 91%?

These silent years of Jesus undoubtedly formed the foundation for the 9%. This is where Jesus grew. Every follower of Jesus and any person who seriously desires to take up the mantle of leading others must also learn to lead themselves. Even though Jesus was God in flesh, He intentionally grew intellectually, physically, spiritually and relationally. If Jesus grew, so should we. Contained with 2:52 lies the blueprint of learning to grow on purpose.

ISBN 978-1-908393-25-8

Published by River Publishing – www.river-publishing.co.uk

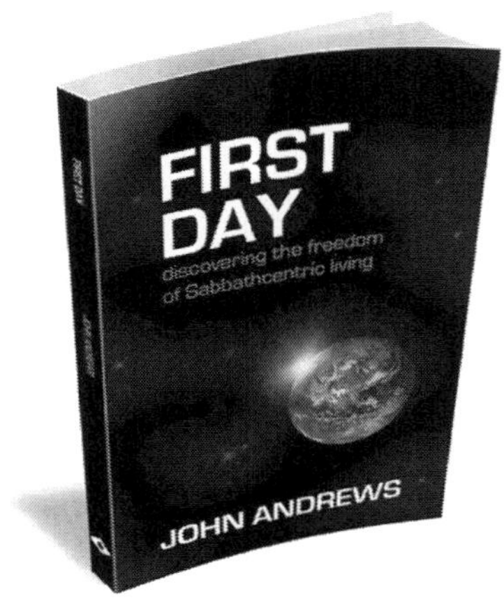

First Day

Discovering the freedom of Sabbathcentric living

John Andrews challenges us to look at our lives in the light of Adam and Eve's "first day" on the planet. Although the Sabbath was "day 7" for God in terms of creation, it was "day 1" for newly created humanity. Before God asked Adam and Eve to "do" anything, He invited them simply to "be" - to enjoy and understand the power of rest.

The Sabbath teaches us the principle of working out of a place of "rest" in God, not simply "resting from work". At it's heart are three vital truths:

- Worship - which is God-centred
- Worth - we are "beings" not "do-ings"
- Work - we work out of a proper understanding of our purpose through a clear insight into our value before God.

The principles contained within the concept of "Sabbath" are not simply intended as a once-per-week experience. Rather, they express a lifestyle that should shape our whole experience of walking with and trusting God.

ISBN 978-1-908393-01-2

Published by River Publishing – www.river-publishing.co.uk

The Real 'F' Word

Forgiveness is one of the greatest words in any language and central to the gospel message. Without forgiveness we are impoverished and alone. Given a chance, this gloriously offensive word will change us as individuals and change the world we inhabit.

ISBN 978-1-905991-45-7

Identity Theft

This book gives insight into how we can discover and protect our identity. Without it we will be defined and controlled by people or circumstances, but with it, we can be more than conquerors.

ISBN 978-1-905991-11-2

Moving Beyond Mediocrity

For every level of breakthrough in life there will be times of challenge. Many factors conspire to prevent us breaking out of our boundaries. But if we are to move beyond mediocrity, we must come to terms with the battle which always accompanies breakthrough.

ISBN 978-1-903725-92-4